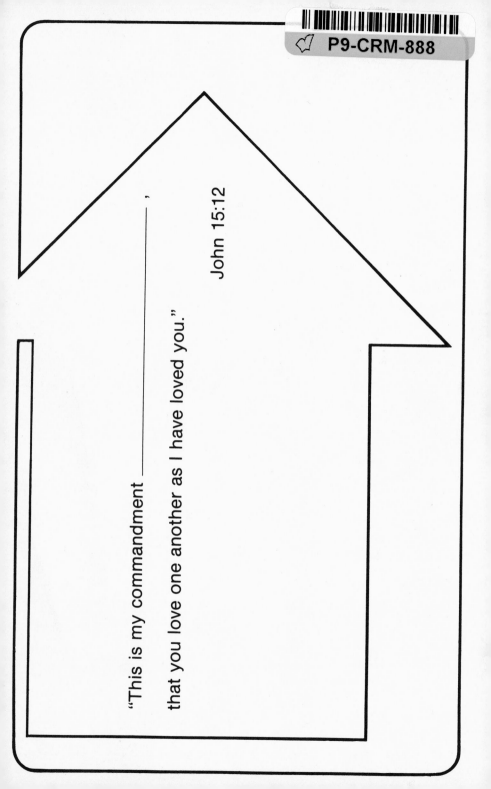

"This is my commandment _____,

that you love one another as I have loved you."

John 15:12

Dear Family

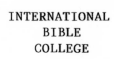

Other books by Zig Ziglar

See You at the Top (1974)
Confessions of a Happy Christian (1978)

Dear Family

ZIG ZIGLAR

Author of SEE YOU AT THE TOP

PELICAN PUBLISHING COMPANY
GRETNA 1984

Library of Congress Cataloging in Publication Data

Ziglar, Zig.
  Dear family.

  1. Family—United States. 2. Family—Religious life.
3. Ziglar, Zig. I. Title.
HQ536.Z47 1984   306.8'5'0924   84-3180
ISBN: 0-88289-416-1

Manufactured in the United States of America
Published by Pelican Publishing Company, Inc.
1101 Monroe Street, Gretna, Louisiana 70053

Dedicated to My Family

CONTENTS

Part II
Love Is

Part III
Rearing Successful, Well-Adjusted Children

Part IV
Courtship, Love, Marriage, and Sex

THANK YOU

As an author, I've often wondered just how much help other writers have received from all the people they recognize in the foreword or in the acknowledgment section of their books. In my case, the assistance I've received has been tremendously helpful, and I'm deeply grateful for the hours invested by my "coauthors" to help make this a more meaningful book.

The first person I recognize is the Redhead—my wife—who spent countless hours in reading, then rereading, and reading again. Not only did she devote a great deal of time, but her insight and suggestions significantly improved the book. She helped me to remember many forgotten things and corrected my memory in other areas when it was faulty. She also saved me some embarrassment by gently suggesting certain changes in phrases, terms, and approaches. As you'll see throughout the book, we have an unusual relationship.

My administrative assistant, Laurie Downing, has been enormously helpful. Her enthusiasm for the work, combined with her capacity to use our word processor at such an incredible speed, has been amazing. In the process of writing, rewriting, then writing again, again, again, and yet again, the patience and persistence of a Laurie Downing cannot be stressed or appreciated enough. Her willingness to express opinions concerning certain facets of the manuscript was also significant. She responded to questions but never volunteered an opinion unless it was sought. Needless to say, that opinion was sought quite often.

My three daughters, Jean Suzanne Witmeyer, Cindy Ann Oates, and Julie Ziglar Norman, as well as my son, Tom, also made valuable contributions. As a matter of fact, they all helped old Dad avoid some serious mistakes, and on many different occasions corrected some areas where my slant and emphasis was off base. They gave their opinions freely and shared some valuable lessons while encouraging me all the way. It's really neat to have four children whom you love and also respect.

The two ladies outside the family who also made invaluable contributions are the wives of the president and the executive vice president of The Zig Ziglar Corporation, Mrs. Anne Ezinga and Mrs. Karen Roossien. They spent more concentrated analytical time on the book than just about anybody. They evaluated and rated each letter, made suggestions for change and improvement, and expressed opinions as to which letters should be excluded.

Jim Savage, our vice president of corporate training, helped put the finishing touches on the book with his unique insights, refinement of terms and phrases, and contribution to punctuation and grammatical accuracy.

I'm also indebted to Psychologist Denis Waitley, my friend and platform associate, for his encouragement and support. His willingness to "check me out" for psychological accuracy was most meaningful, especially as it relates to the comments on television and MTV.

Three other people who were extremely helpful with the book are Dave and Marilyn Bauer, independent contractors in charge of our computer programs, and Ralph Tanner, the husband of Mrs. Linda Tanner, our office manager. These three evaluated the letters on a scale of one to ten and expressed opinions as to which letters should be deleted. The opinions they rendered were the determining factor in several cases.

I would also like to thank Dr. Forest Tennant, General Robinson Risner, Dr. Richard Furman, Jim Janz, Tammy Johnson, Thomas G. and Tom Kamp, Steve Smith, and the Martin Lovvorn family for permitting me to use their stories and suggestions.

Additionally, I would like to express a heartfelt "thank you" to the other members of our outstanding staff who shouldered many additional responsibilities while I was busy writing *Dear Family.*

Dear Family

INTRODUCTION

This is a book of letters. Many were actually written. Some were not. All of them should have been written because each letter comes from my heart and expresses my feelings toward my family. As I share these thoughts, many of which I have never shared before, *I do so with the hope that you will get some thoughts or ideas that will draw you closer to your own family and make your life more meaningful and rewarding.*

I'd be less than candid if I failed to confess that time has dulled my memory, and that my nature is such that I tend to remember the pleasant and positive aspects of life while relegating the negative events to secondary positions. There are occasions when I fear I will come across as a "goody-goody" husband and father with a goody-goody wife, goody-goody children, and goody-goody grandchildren. That is not my intention because we, too, have had our problems.

My wife and I, especially in the early years of our marriage, had our share of differences and difficulties. Each one of our children has at one time or another rebelled in a minor or even significant way. Each of our girls did cause us considerable pain, and some tears were shed as a result. We take much comfort in the old saying that "all's well that ends well." First, the tears they brought were few compared to the joy and

3

laughter they've brought into our lives; and second, I don't believe there is a mother or a daddy anywhere who could be any more proud of and grateful for their children than we are of ours.

Most importantly, to be candid, much of any difficulty and grief we had was largely because I did not assume the spiritual leadership in my family until my youngest daughter was seventeen. Consequently, our daughters missed the spiritual direction our son has benefitted from since he was seven. Each of our children received a lot of love, discipline, and attention, and some church attendance was required, but real spiritual guidance, especially from me, was missing. Fortunately, each one of our children enjoys a personal relationship with Jesus Christ today.

This tells us several things. First, it says that parents can do the right things as far as loving their children and exposing them to the right values and attitudes and still have some grief. This also tells us that we must not give up on our children, *especially* if they rebel and cause heartache. This behavior could be a sign that our children have given up on themselves and feel they don't "deserve" our love or share our expectations for them. Our love and belief in them could be all they have to hang onto. Let's not let them down.

Our family, like most families, is made up of individuals, and we are all real and quite imperfect, but the statement that "love is blind" is at least partially true in my case. My perspective might be at least mildly influenced by my love for them and my gratitude to God for each one of them. I mention this because my daughters have each told me that my relationship with their mother is at least "unusual," and that I have a tendency to overlook their faults and indiscretions while coming across to them as a shining knight on a white horse who could do no wrong. My! My!

As a matter of fact, daughter Suzan recently confided that it wasn't until she was a young teenager that she fully understood that her parents were even slightly less than perfect. (These kids will eventually find you out, won't they?) Since she had been measuring herself against "perfection" until that time, it was a great confidence-builder when she learned that her parents had shortcomings, but still managed to survive and even make progress.

Having said that, let me point out that I can honestly say the experience of preparing this manuscript has heightened my love for my family and brought me even closer to them. As I express these thoughts and feelings, it crystallizes my thinking and especially calls attention to what an incredibly fortunate man I am.

How blessed I am that God saw fit to make for me the special woman He did; how He blessed our relationship with four beautiful, healthy children, three fine sons-in-law, and now four magnificent granddaughters* and a fantastic grandson. I will also confess that my resolution to be a better husband, father, brother, grandfather, and father-in-law is reaffirmed.

I would suspect that many who read these words have been equally blessed, but for whatever reason have never fully expressed their love and gratitude. I encourage you not to let another day go by that you don't verbally and physically express to your family how much you really do love them and how much they mean to you. To steal a line from the success book in the business world, *DO IT NOW!*

If you're not the kind of person who can express yourself verbally, then the written word is a marvelous way to communicate. For one thing, you have a chance to finish your thoughts without fear of embarrassment or interruption. As

---

*On Friday, December 9, 1983, at precisely 11:16 A.M., weighing in at six pounds, fourteen and one-half ounces and measuring nineteen and one-half inches, to the obvious joy and delight of her grandparents (actually, Suzan and Chad were glad, too!), Suzan Elizabeth Wescott Witmeyer made a belated but *most* welcome appearance.

you express your thoughts, the lift you give that family member to whom you write could make *the* difference.

In a world where so many people are constantly being "put down," where negativism prevails, sin abounds, and discouragement surrounds some members of the family, your note or word of encouragement could make a world of difference. Many times people ask, "What can I do?" and often ask the question rhetorically, not expecting an answer.

I can tell you that one of the things you can do today is to express to your family members your gratitude, pride, and love for them and how much you enjoy being with them. As you express these thoughts in writing, you will be amazed at what it does for your attitude and how much more real all of these facts become. DO IT NOW. The benefits are enormous, and if you do so, you will never have to say "I wish I had."

PART I

THE ZIGLAR CLAN

Note! *Just in case you skipped the introduction as being irrelevant, unimportant, or worse—uninteresting—let me encourage you to go back and read it. It does much to set the tone of the book.*

THE ZIGLAR CLAN

Dear Reader,

I'd like to introduce you to my family and share some stories with you so you can better understand where I'm coming from.

I start with my wife, who is the most important person in my life. Her name is Jean. When I talk to her, she's "Sugar Baby," and when I talk about her, she's "the Redhead." Many of the letters are to her, but I believe this one will give you a clear idea why I'm so grateful God gave her to me on November 26, 1946.

A BEAUTIFUL MOMENT

Dear Sugar Babe and all other romanticists,

Over the years we've had so many beautiful moments that it's difficult to pick out the most beautiful. However, I believe I can do exactly that.

About three years after I committed my life to Christ, we had gotten up reasonably early one morning and were seated at the little table in our bedroom, having a cup of coffee. We weren't doing much talking, but we were holding hands, which is fairly standard for our early-morning rendezvous when we seem to concentrate on enjoying each other's presence. That morning as we sat there, you looked at me and said, "You know, Honey, I wish I were younger." To this I responded, "For goodness' sake, why?" Your answer is indelibly burned into my mind. You looked at me, smiled, and said, "If I were younger, I could be your wife even longer."

I'll have to confess, Sweetheart, that those words moved me as no words moved me before or since. I've never felt more loved or more like we were one than at that particular moment. That says a lot, because we've certainly had more than our share of special moments. We've been to many places and shared many exciting experiences, but in the final analysis, the one that meant the most to me was the one in our own home, on that beautiful morning.

Your loving husband,

ZIG

Thought: *Love and happiness are not found in those faraway places with strange-sounding names. Love is found in the care, consideration, and presence of your mate on a daily basis.*

The person who influenced my life most as far as my education and character are concerned was my mother. Even though she only finished the fifth grade, she was the wisest person and greatest teacher I've ever known. By word and deed she taught with hundreds of little "sermonettes" that creep into my conversations, speeches, and writings to this day.

Mother carried an incredible work-load and responsibilities

that were brought about by the death of my father, which left her with six children who were either too young to work or still in school. To compound her heartache, she lost her thirteen-month-old baby girl a week later. Despite this double tragedy and the grief involved, my mother never indulged herself in self-pity or bitterness. In her case, grief and self-pity were luxuries she could not afford. Her other children, Judge, 3, Zig, 5, Howard, 9, Evia, 12, Huel, 15, and Turah, 17, as well as the older ones (there were twelve of us), needed her love, attention, and strength. Even with milking and caring for five cows, working a large garden, canning over a hot wood stove, washing by hand, and quilting until all hours of the night, she still took time to bake us cakes and pies. More importantly, she gave us time and affection. That's love.

I never heard my mother say an unkind thing about anyone else, and when any member of the family stumbled and got into trouble (yes, we had problems, too), mother was always there to defend and help the fallen one. She hated sin, but she was not judgmental. She loved the sinner and always knew that with God's grace he could rise above it. That's love.

The next letter expresses some of my love for my mother and, I hope, will offer a thought or two that will be helpful to you.

GIVE UP SOME THINGS EARLY—GAIN GREATER BENEFITS LATER

Dear Mama and everybody else,

I know you will never read these words, but since I said these things to you when you were alive, I feel comfortable in committing them to print in the hope that another mother's son or daughter somewhere might also benefit from your wisdom.

Remember, Mama, how from time to time you would say you regretted that your children had to work so hard when we were small? You regretted it because you felt we had missed an important portion of our childhood. There were occasions when I would have preferred playing with my friends instead of working in the grocery store, but none of us resented having to work, Mama, because your hard-working, loving example made anything we did look minute by comparison. I know you're at peace on that issue today, but I wanted to get it on the record so others might benefit and know what a remarkable mama I had.

In my professional life I teach a lot of people how to set goals, and I always explain that in order to get something you must exchange something for it. When I think of all I gained, what I "gave up" pales in comparison.

I gained the privilege of learning to work and of accepting responsibility at an early age, so I got a real jump on the boys and girls in my age group. I learned self-reliance and how to be self-supporting, while learning the basic principles of life in the business community. I learned self-discipline and many other things, Mama, that many boys and girls don't learn until they are adults. What an advantage this gave me when I started my full-time work, my marriage, and my family.

I hasten to add that all of your children understood that our jobs helped provide the necessities of life, and the earnings were not spent on frivolous things. I'm confident you would not have *permitted* us to work if our goal had been to buy fancy clothes or cars or anything else that would have moved us into the adult world before we were mature enough to handle it.

I always loved you, Mama, and because you told me of your love so many times, I frequently told you of mine. But there's no way I can tell you, in looking back over the years, how much I appreciate the fact that you gave me a chance as a young boy to learn how to support myself and make a contribution to others. The lesson was invaluable. I gave up so little and gained so much!

Your loving son,

HILARY

Message: *Teach your child today, in a loving way, what he* needs *to know for a better tomorrow — and he will surely love you tomorrow — as he does today!*

Directly and indirectly, the impact of my wife's mother and dad on my life was considerable. Jean, too, comes from a very loving family. Her dad died when she was only ten years old, but she vividly remembers him as a loving, affectionate daddy with a good sense of humor who took advantage of every opportunity to spend time with his family. Mr. Abernathy, better known as "Mr. Ab," was the first Boy Scout executive in the state of Mississippi. This letter to him shows how today's actions can and do affect tomorrow's lives.

Dear Mr. Ab,

I never met you, but your youngest daughter has told me a great deal about you. It wasn't until recently that I really came to appreciate the kind of man you were and the impact you had *and are still having*. Your life confirms the old saying, "Bread cast upon the waters will come back buttered."

Here are the circumstances. While doing a film on my life, we invited a former teacher who had considerable impact on me, Coach Joby Harris of Hinds Junior College in Raymond, Mississippi, to participate. You undoubtedly will remember him, Mr. Ab, because as his scoutmaster you spent a great deal of time with him. As a twelve-year-old, Joby Harris was in your troop. Coach Harris told me that you were like a second father to him and that you had a great deal of influence in helping him to mold and shape his life.

Twenty-five years later, Joby Harris was Coach Harris at Hinds Junior College, and I was a student in his class. Never will I forget that first session. I was taking American history, not because I wanted to, but because it was required for me to graduate. I honestly felt that history was a waste of time. At the end of that class, however, I was a history major. Coach Harris had thoroughly sold me on knowing my history, on waving our flag, and on the free enterprise system. He was tremendously influential in "selling" me on taking an active part in doing something about making America an even better place in which to live.

Actually, much of my interest in people today and my philosophy of life was influenced enormously by Coach Harris. I honestly feel that Coach Harris helped to make me a better man and, hence, a better husband—for your daughter.

I know Mr. Ab, that since you went to be with the Lord many years ago, you knew all of this before I did. I just wanted to put it in the record that the good each individual can do today will live on and on and on. That's the reason many of us believe that our Lord does not judge us upon the day of our death, but waits that one thousand years. I don't know you yet, Mr. Ab, but I sure do love you.

Your son-in-law,

ZIG ZIGLAR

When Mr. Ab died, Jean's mother sold the family car and, with the life insurance money he had left her, elected to stay home and spend every possible moment raising and educating her children. This was a decision she never regretted.

As the youngest one (that was my Redhead) was starting the tenth grade, Mrs. Ab went to work outside the home for the first time. To this day the Redhead still talks about the fact that her mother was there to send her off to school and to welcome her home every day. She feels that the benefits from a love-and-security point of view far exceeded any of the "things" her mother might have bought her by taking a job outside the home.

By no stretch of imagination am I trying to hang a "guilt trip" on those countless mothers who *must* work to provide the necessities of life for their children. I am simply expressing the feelings my wife and I, as well as our children, have about having had our mothers at home.

Mrs. Ab was a warm, loving, and affectionate mother, mother-in-law, and grandmother. She, too, was "old-fashioned" as far as her faith and moral values were concerned. She had a strong sense of fairness and what was "right," but most of all she had a compelling love for her family and communicated that love every day in every way.

Mrs. Ab and I hit it off from the very first. Deep down, I think she knew from about the second time she ever saw me that I was eventually going to "ride off into the sunset" with her youngest daughter. I'll always be grateful that I had a chance to spend as much time with her as I did and regretful that the time frame wasn't even greater.

My, how she loved her children and grandchildren! What a joy it was to watch her face light up when she hugged and kissed them. She has gone home to her eternal reward, so I'm confident she is peeking down from time to time, watching her grandchildren and great-grandchildren as they grow and develop.

Dear Family is a book with several objectives, but the underlying purpose is to reinforce and strengthen the American family, which is under serious attack and is faltering badly in many areas (divorce, wife and child abuse, family rape and incest, abortion, and attempts by some radical groups to redefine the family as "two or more adults living together").

This letter to my daughter deals with the subject of working mothers.

IF YOU CAN, MOM, STAY AT HOME

Dear Suzan—and all other "stay-at-home-to-raise-the-children" mothers,

You're one of the lucky ones, and I'm sure you know that. In today's society, financial necessity forces a high percentage of mothers into the job market. You, on the other hand, are able to stay at home and give your time and love to Katherine Jean Alexandra Witmeyer, better known as "Keeper." That's beautiful. Even more beautiful is the fact that you are happy in that choice.

I believe you are wise to do without some of the luxuries to spend that time with your baby during her formative years. As you know, a child's personality and moral values are largely developed by the time he or she is five years old.

One of the major problems in our society today is that many people often try to make mothers who "*just* raise their children" feel like second-class citizens. That's tragic — and grossly unfair, because the most important job in our society is raising our children to be loving, responsible, moral, law-abiding citizens. Evidence is solid that children who have that extra time and attention from their mothers have a better chance for a happy childhood and a successful life.

If a mother chooses to work, that's her privilege. If she has to work, that's her responsibility. But, if she has the freedom to stay at home and raise her children, she deserves praise and recognition, not ridicule and criticism. America's desperate need now is to have more mothers (and fathers, too) spending more time with their children. Again, I'm delighted to know you're staying at home to raise my grand-daughter and the future grandchildren you and Chad will present to us.

Love,

DAD

The next letter reaffirms the beauty and benefits which can come from a loving family.

Dear brothers, sisters, brothers-in-law, and sisters-in-law,

How sad that so many people today are not fortunate enough to have a loving family to share their love! How unfortunate that many families who love each other don't take the time or opportunity to express that love! With that in mind, I want to take time to share with our readers how special you are and how much your love has meant to me.

I start with Lera, my oldest sister, whose loving nature, combined with the respect and concern she showed for our mother, is firmly embedded in my memory.

Along these lines, surely one of the most beautiful demonstrations of love I have ever witnessed was the devotion showered upon my mother in the declining years of her life by my three other sisters and their husbands.

I begin with sister Turah and her husband, Weldon Allen. Mother spent the last twelve years of her life with them, and two years of that time she was confined to her bed. During this time Turah and Weldon bathed, petted, cared for, and generally spoiled her in every way you could spoil one of God's special servants. Every day Turah brushed her hair and gave her a full beauty treatment. *Nobody* ever visited mother those last few years of her life who did not comment on her hair, which had almost no gray, and her complexion, which was beautiful and without wrinkles until she quietly closed her eyes at age eighty-seven and found her eternal peace.

In many ways I suppose we could "expect" Turah to be that loving and caring for our mother, but in my book, Weldon Allen rates a special place in the hall of fame when it comes to pure love. I've often said to him that the love and care he gave my mother during the last few years of her life far exceeded anything any male member of the family gave to her. I also recall those countless hours they spent working out in the garden when Mama was still up and around. Mama was the supervisor and Allen did the work. Allen maintains that he was the biggest winner in the relationship and since Mama led him to know Jesus Christ as Lord, I'm sure that's true, but his devotion to and care for my mother could only have come from a heart filled with love.

Actually, the caring for Mother was a team effort in every

sense of the word. Sister Evia Jane, who is a practical nurse, pushed herself far beyond her physical limitations as she made several trips each week from her home in Jackson, Mississippi, to help care for the mother she so deeply loved. Incidentally, Evia Jane, along with my other brothers and sisters, is quite an inspiration. She undoubtedly had one of the most difficult lives I've ever witnessed. Yet, her indomitable spirit and will never wavered. She worked incredibly hard and sacrificed a great deal for her children, but the results speak for themselves.

What a thrill it was for all of us when she married A. P. Lindsey. What a marvelous move that was on both their parts! A. P. has humored, babied, and catered to her, and she's done exactly the same thing for him. How great it is to see the two of them together and to know that after years of toil and turmoil she married such a good and Godly man.

Rounding out the "love-care" team was sister Lola who left her home in Columbus, Georgia, and moved in with Turah and Weldon for fourteen months to help care for Mama. Needless to say, her contribution was monumental.

Interestingly enough, when you talk to Turah, Weldon, Evia Jane, A. P., and Lola about their devotion and "sacrifice," they pooh-pooh the idea. Instead, they each speak in glowing terms about the privilege they had in serving Mama those last few years of her life. That's love.

My two oldest brothers (twins) have always been an inspiration and ideal role models. Huie had such a beautiful and humble spirit and entertained all of us with stories of his "talking dogs." Our girls especially remember how they loved to visit Uncle Huie and Aunt Jewel because they could gather eggs, ride the horse, and generally take over the place. Cousin Earl was their constant companion, and his untimely death in an automobile accident left us all in shocked grief for a long time. The biggest thing the family remembers about Uncle Huie and Aunt Jewel is their absolute joy at having any of their kinfolks visit them!*

In many ways brother Hubert is the best and most unusual man I have ever known. For fifteen years he regularly visited and taught a Sunday school lesson to an invalid who couldn't go to church, and none of us ever knew. He smiles and says that it gave him practice for his regular class. I'm confident that when the roll is called up yonder many limelight Christians will be seated behind this brother of mine who labored quietly, but whose love and servant's heart cast a giant shadow. The Lord will surely greet him with, "Well done, thou good and faithful servant!"

It wasn't a big deal, but brother Howard certainly scored lots of points with me on at least one occasion. Never will I forget "that day," some thirty-nine years ago, when I was a student at Hinds Junior College in Raymond, Mississippi. I received a money order for ten dollars. Howard was in the Navy and his monthly checks were only about sixty dollars, so for him to squeeze out ten dollars and send it to me was really an effort! I was "destitute" when the ten dollars arrived. Since you could buy an ice cream sundae for fifteen cents and a malted milk for twenty cents, that ten dollars represented untold wealth to me. His untimely death at age forty-two eliminated the possibility of my children really getting to know him.

Had the name *Huckleberry Finn* not already been taken, I'm certain that brother Huel would have ended up with that one. When he saw two youngsters fighting, he would automatically challenge the winner of the fight to do battle with me. Never will I forget one challenge he issued on my behalf

---

*On October 7, 1983, brother Huie quietly closed his eyes and went Home to be with the Lord he loved so much and served so faithfully. On January 18, 1984, his twin brother Hubert joined him in Paradise.

to a bigger guy when I was in the sixth grade. We went at it pretty good during the lunch break and that afternoon met about three blocks from school, in front of Mitchell's Barber Shop on Canal Street. In the case of small boys, the one who gets in a lucky blow is generally the one who wins. As luck would have it, I got in one of those licks and the fight was all over—and was I ever glad!

Just as the fight ended, my teacher, Mrs. Worley, arrived on the scene. She proceeded to take all of us to task, but especially big brother Huel. She asked him if he had seen the fight, and he courteously and enthusiastically replied, "Yes, M'am, I sure did!" She then demanded to know why he had not stopped it. His answer was a classic: "Shucks, Mrs. Worley, there wasn't any need to stop the fight. My brother was winning!"

In the truest sense, that's what families are for—to look after and take up for each other. But I hasten to add that this does not include getting your brother into fights!

My youngest brother is known as "Judge" on the speaking circuit, but to me he has been and always will be "Hoss." I suppose the thing my children will remember most about Hoss is the fact that he has always been so deeply interested in each one of them and has always given them an extra-special amount of attention.

Brother Houston was the primary breadwinner for many years after Dad died, and helped provide us with food, clothing, and shelter. My children did not get to know him very well because of his premature death from emphysema. As he lay in the hospital month after month, fighting for every breath of air, one of the most inspiring sights I've ever seen was the devotion of his wife, Nellie, who was there day after day, month after month. If there's ever been a good example of faithfulness and devotion, this was it.

In concluding this letter, I want to make certain my brothers, sisters, brothers-in-law, and sisters-in-law know how much I love and appreciate them.

Love,

ZIG ZIGLAR

Since I've already written a lot about love, and since I will write even more about it, perhaps it would be appropriate to insert a love letter at this point.

LOVE IS A BAKED SWEET POTATO

Dear Sugar Babe,

In my own way I've tried to tell you in every way I know that I love you. As I sat down to write this letter the thought occurred to me that most people do not know what real love is. With this in mind, I decided that since there are so many ideas and opinions about what love is, I could help clear the air so others might have a better understanding. That's important, because in today's society there is much confusion on the subject of love—with many of our young people confusing sex and love and thinking a "meaningful relationship" parallels a total commitment to a lifetime mate. For this reason, I wanted to put on paper some thoughts that have been on my mind and in my heart for a long time.

From time to time, I see on the screen or on the cover of a magazine headlines claiming something to the effect that "this story is the greatest love story ever told." Unfortunately, in too many of these cases they are talking about a pornographic display of illicit passion. Obviously, one of these days somebody will tell the greatest love story ever told, but that is all it will be—the greatest love story ever *told.* It certainly will not be the greatest love story ever, because no man or woman deeply committed to each other within the bonds of holy matrimony would ever share the intimate details of their love with even one other person, because to do so would cheapen their love and make it common.

It is my strong, personal conviction that love is a baked sweet potato. In my mind, a sweet potato about the size of a man's fist, which has been baked in a moderately hot oven so that the skin does not dry out and puff up, is ideal. The skin needs to be soft and pliable because it, too, is delicious and should be eaten with considerable relish.

Visualize, if you will, taking that beautiful potato out of the oven, slitting it down the middle, and heaping gobs of pure butter (margarine just won't do!) into that potato so that every nook and cranny is saturated. To add *anything* other than butter would amount to sacrilege!

The baked sweet potato, to be completely enjoyed, must be eaten separately, or as dessert. Before you take the first bite, you must rinse your mouth with cool water so your taste buds will be alive and popping. For the first couple of bites you close your eyes and savor the delicious flavor. Slowly you let it melt until every fiber of your being becomes aware of the superb taste of the potato. I am convinced that the baked sweet potato is truly a food fit for kings. It is beyond my wildest imagination to conceive of anyone not going into ecstasy at the very thought of eating one!

Incredibly enough, Sweetheart, even though you have been mine for over thirty-seven years, you still do not really enjoy baked sweet potatoes. I cannot imagine such a condition prevailing in any home, much less in my own, but that's the way it is. So, when I come home and catch the unparalleled, distinctive, mouthwatering, and almost maddening aroma of a baked sweet potato in all its intensity, my thoughts turn to love. I know that when you went to the store you were thinking about me. When you brought that sweet potato home and washed it, you were thinking about me. When you slipped it into the oven, you were thinking about me. And when you placed it on the table you were thinking about me.

Now I know some who read this will undoubtedly think, "But, Zig, a baked sweet potato is such a little thing!" Realistically, I agree that a baked sweet potato might be a "little thing." However, I must ask the obvious question: Isn't that what love is all about? Isn't it a series of "little things" done for someone else for no reason other than the fact that you love them? Yes, love is revealed in the countless little things that take place every day in our lives. I'm convinced that if every married person would give their mate a "baked sweet potato" every day in the form of little courtesies and considerations, many marriages would move from the rocks to the clouds. Sure do love you, Sweetheart.

ZIG

Question: *What "little thing" have you done today to show your love for your mate? Remember, it's the little things you do every day that bring you closer and closer every year and make the love stories of thirty, forty, fifty, and sixty years' duration truly "The Greatest Love Story Ever Lived."*

Dear Reader,

Since I talked about love so much in my last letter to you as a reader, I feel it is important to understand the importance of time as it often relates to the love and closeness we feel for our families. Countless studies reveal that the television set is viewed over six hours daily in the average American home. Other studies by the University of Pennsylvania and the

National Parent-Teacher Association reveal that average American parents spend approximately seven and one-half minutes *per week* talking with their children. (I'm not talking about eating or watching television with your children. I'm talking about talking *with* them.) *And* much of that time is instructional ("Be sure to feed the cat." "Don't forget your coat").

I firmly believe that if you will take the next letter to heart, you could put this book down at that point and you will have gotten far more than your money's worth.

Sincerely,

ZIG ZIGLAR

Dear Ziglar Children,

I believe the two most destructive words ever put together in tandem are the words "quality time." Behind these two words millions of husbands and wives who spend very little time with each other will hide and say, "We don't have much time together, but it's 'quality' time." Parents do the same thing.

I'm grateful that as a young father I felt impelled to spend not only quality time, but quantity time, with each one of you. As you girls reached the age of six months, I would take you to the grocery store to do the shopping. I was in the cookware business, and each day I had to buy food for the demonstrations I conducted each evening. We spent lots of time together, and I had a chance to play with you, love you, talk to you, and show you off. I was very proud, and never missed an opportunity to let people see how bright and pretty you were.

When you came along ten years later, Tom, we had a chance to do a lot of things together. I well recall that when we moved to Dallas you were only three-and-a-half years old.

There were some woods near our house and we spent a lot of time there. We'd walk around and spend an hour or two together. We'd always end up under the same old oak tree where we sat and talked about anything and everything. I know you remember the day we saw the mother raccoon and her three little ones. That was perhaps the highlight of all our trips down there. Of course, we discovered new paths, secret hiding places, hidden trails, and lots of other neat things. Most of all, Son, we had a chance to spend that time together and get acquainted. I think it set the stage for our relationship today.

You girls will remember that when you got to be about six years old, one by one I would take you on my trips. By then I was working in both North and South Carolina, and we'd stay gone two or three days. You had a chance to go into the hotels and motels and restaurants; you met the men and women your dad worked with. Best of all, on those long trips we had a chance to talk. I believe that's one of the reasons that today we call each other and visit regularly about things that are important, as well as things that are trivial.

Like most fathers it was my happy privilege to have the "fun" times with all of you. That's not to say I didn't accept *some* of the routine and unpleasant responsibilities that came my way, like getting up at night to give you an occasional 2:00 A.M. bottle, or to take you to the bathroom. However, when you get down to the nitty-gritty, it was always your mother who changed the dirty diapers. It was your mother who rocked you and cared for you when you were sick. It was your mother who spent those countless hours reading you stories and helping you with your homework. It was your mother who brushed away the tears, kissed away the hurts, hugged away your friends' rejections, settled the disputes with your siblings, and served as the disciplinarian in about 93 percent of the cases. In short, your mother was always there.

Of all the little things I did, the things your mother seemed to appreciate the most were those middle-of-the-night trips to the bathroom, as well as the restroom trips when we were occasionally indulging ourselves in a meal in a restaurant. I'm confident this was because she rarely, if ever, in those early years, was able to eat a meal without interruption or to sleep all night without having to get up.

In our conversations today, I'm pleased to say that we touch on all the subjects that are important in life, from salvation to raising your children. You name it, and we talk about it. That's good. I believe our closeness today is possible and enjoyable because when you were small we spent a lot of time together. As you raise your families, I urge you to make time to spend with your little ones. They grow up so fast, and they're gone before you know it.

Love,

DAD

Thought: *There are exceptions to every rule, but by and large you* will *spend time with your children. You will* invest *that time with them when they are young, teaching them sound moral values so you can enjoy them when they get older, or you will* spend *time with them when they are older, counseling them and bailing them out of trouble.*

Dear Reader,

The Redhead and I feel especially blessed with three outstanding sons-in-law. Not only is each one of them much-loved and appreciated as an individual, but as a group they are such a delight to be around. Naturally, I feel that all of them are "over-married," but since I did the same thing, I can't help but love and admire them for their good taste, judgment, and high standards.

The first one to smooth-talk his way into the family circle was Richard Oates, who married Cindy. Very few people would argue with the observation that Richard is one of the sweetest, most lovable guys anybody could find. He's always upbeat, and always a joy to be with and around.

Chad Witmeyer was the second one to enter our family. Since he and Suzan walked down the aisle, it has been a real pleasure for me to be able to spend time with Chad, both as a member of the family and as the manager of the audio and video duplication production facility at our company. When I watch Chad and little Keeper playing by the hour in the swimming pool, I marvel at the stamina of both and am impressed with what a good daddy Chad is!

Rounding out the team is Jim Norman, who only recently joined the family. What an exciting addition he has been! How great to see the care and love he showers on our daughter, Julie, and "Sunshine." How neat it is to see how beautifully and completely he fits into the family with his children, Cheryl, Jim, and Jenny. And that, of course, gives us THREE more grandchildren to love!

Finishing up the list of kinfolks I want to talk about is Brother Bern. He's not a blood brother, but in every other way he is a brother. He is the incurable optimist, the incredible hard-worker, the beautifully organized and the extraordinarily bright businessman who just happened to love me as a brother and my children almost as he loved his own.

The next letter reveals why Brother Bern rates so high on my totem pole.

Dear Brother Bern:

I suppose that over the years you and I have spent more time together than I have spent with most of my natural-born brothers. This is certainly true after I became a man. You've played an important part in my life, Brother Bern. The belief you had in me as a speaker was a strong sustaining force for several years when I had those serious doubts in my own mind as to whether I would ever make it in this field. Your willingness to share with me and believe in me was always astonishing and encouraging.

How well I remember when you first started using me as a speaker. You not only paid me my regular fee, but you always had two new suits waiting for me at the convention. I would mildly protest, but you always pointed out that you had gotten two suits exactly like those you gave me because you were hoping that people would get us confused and think you were Zig Ziglar. Of course, we both knew it was a pure "con" job. You knew that my career was not going well and as a speaker I needed to be professionally dressed. But you always made me feel like I was the one doing you the favor. That's what being a brother is all about, Brother Bern.

Oh, you did other things, too. You bailed me out of a couple of serious financial jams, and you did it in a way that enabled me to maintain my pride and dignity. You flew to Dallas on two different occasions to help me with some business decisions, and you spent two days with me in New York on an important matter. Through the years I always knew you were there. Thank you for being a brother, Brother Bern.

BROTHER ZIG

That's the Ziglar family. If we were to get involved in all the cousins, uncles, aunts, and their children this would be a 4,000-page book. But I want to say that I'm proud to be a Ziglar, proud and grateful to have the wife, children, grandchildren, sons-in-law, brothers, sisters, nieces, and nephews whom I have.

Sincerely,

ZIG ZIGLAR

Dear Reader:

I conclude this segment on the Ziglar clan with a letter our son Tom wrote to Jean and me one Sunday morning. As a threesome, we had enjoyed a particularly meaningful couple of days together. Tom handed us this letter when we sat down in the sanctuary of the church a few minutes before the worship services started. We knew of Tom's love for our Lord and his love for us, but we were hardly prepared for his capacity to express that love with such spiritual depth and eloquence. I'm confident the people around us wondered what was going on as the three of us sat there with tears streaming down our cheeks, attempting to embrace each other without creating a scene. Yes, God has been good to me and mine.

Mom and Dad,

Thank you so much for everything, Mom. Christmas was great! I love *everything* I got so much. I only wish I could give you that much and much, much more. But I don't love the gifts. I love the giver—you. God has blessed us so much, and me because of you, that my only prayer is that our spirits will become humble before God, dwelling on His love and strength and not His gifts.

Dad, you don't know how much our time together means to me. The golf trips will always be something special in my heart in life. I only hope I can treat my kids (Lord willing) the same way. Everything you give, I like. The coat and the money and letting me use your clothes make me so happy. I only wish I could express my joy better when you give them to me. I want you to know that I think of them often and my love for you grows each time because the undeserved gift is the best of all.

I will always love you, but remember that only through God will this love remain perfect. My prayer for us and our family is that God will be the center of our desire. As humans we make mistakes, but God is faithful and just to forgive sins. So when times seem trying, trust God, for through Him everything will be right again.

All my love in Christ for you,

TOM

Part II

LOVE IS

SIXTH GRADERS CAN
BE GREAT TEACHERS

Dear Tom,

I sat in the audience today and listened to the introduction your principal was giving. It was unusual, to say the least. In the beginning I was puzzled as to what he was doing, but when it really hit me, I was moved in a way I am seldom moved.

He said these words:

> Today I'm going to depart from the norm, and instead of telling you a lot about our speaker, I'm going to tell you about a little boy in the sixth grade who sits on the end row, second seat from the back. He's quiet, but in his own way he provides considerable leadership. When a newcomer joins the class, this little boy is always the one who greets him, verbally puts his arm around him, and lets him know that he has a friend in the class. If the youngster is not part of the group, he is the one to include him in activities and make him feel an important part of the process.
>
> Just recently a classmate was told by the doctor that he mustn't attempt to play ball because his vision was so poor he could not see well enough to catch the ball and might get hurt. I looked out on the schoolground and saw our little hero playing catch with this boy. First he stood very, very close, a distance of only a few feet. As the sight-impaired youngster's confidence grew and he could catch the

ball, our hero moved a few steps back until the youngster was catching the ball like the other kids. Yes, our hero is a most unusual little boy, and his daddy is going to be our speaker this morning. Ladies and gentlemen, let's welcome Zig Ziglar.

I'll tell you, Son, no daddy or speaker ever had a better introduction. You probably don't remember it, but your dad was caught speechless for a few moments. Yes, I am proud to be Tom Ziglar's dad.

Love,

DAD

Thought: *Children taught positive values can have a positive, life-changing effect on others around them.*

LOVE IS . . . GIVING A GRANDDAUGHTER A BATH

Dear Keeper (and all other children and grandchildren too young to read),

Obviously you are not old enough to read this because you're only two-and-a-half, and are you ever a fun little girl to have around! At this time, Keeper, perhaps I should explain to you and our readers how you got your name.

When fishermen go fishing and pull in "a nice one," they often say, "That's a keeper!" Well, Keeper, the first time your Granddad laid eyes on you he said to himself, "Now, there's a keeper!" and your name was born. Nothing has ever happened and nothing ever will happen to make your grandparents or your parents change that feeling.

You spent last weekend with Sugar Baby and me, and we had a ball! The highlight of the weekend occurred on the last night after a busy day—and every day for you, Keeper, is "busy." You only have two positions—off and on. When you are "on," you are wide open—no slow-downs, no stops or cautions. It's full-speed ahead. When you are "off," you're really out of it! Incredibly enough, you can switch from either speed to the other in something less than two seconds.

On that last night I gave you your bath. At two-and-a-half, it's really something to watch you as you splash, play, and laugh. With you, Keeper, everything in the bathtub is funny. That night I had to wash your hair, and sometimes this poses a real challenge. When I asked you if you would like for me to turn on the shower, you laughingly agreed. Watching you catch your breath and laugh while the water was rinsing the shampoo out of your hair was an absolute delight.

When I lifted you out of the tub, set you on the towel, dried you off, and dressed you, the way you were hugging and kissing me was so neat!

Just thought you'd like to know how you got your name and how much fun it is to have you around.

Love,

GRANDDADDY

Message: *For some of you, giving my granddaughter a bath might not rate very high on the "Learning/Lesson" scale. If that's your thought, you missed a critical point. If parents and grandparents are going to build meaningful, lifetime relationships with their children, it will require lots of time eating together, reading stories, taking baths and walks, and talking together. You build trust and love with lots of time and care. Each episode might be relatively insignificant, but when you put them all together it means that communication lines will always be open, and the family—all of it—will grow and stay closer together.*

Thought: *Keeper will go through life knowing how much she means to all of us. She will* know *that not only is she a "Keeper," but she is also a winner.*

Fact: *A child's name and nickname can and does mean a lot. Make certain that the "handle" you place on your child is positive* and *loving.*

WHADDAYADO WHEN KIDS' BEHAVIOR CHANGES?

Dear Julie (and all other young parents),

As you remember, about a year ago we had quite a discussion about our concern for Amanda's behavior, especially her irritability and sudden refusal to have anything to do with me. As you undoubtedly remember, you, your mother, and I discussed it in detail. Your mother made a couple of observations which I thought were rather astute. She pointed out a couple of reasons why Amanda Gail might be as irritable and difficult to get along with as she had suddenly become. Your mother felt that Amanda might not be getting enough sleep and that she was eating a lot of junk food loaded with sugar. At that point your mother suggested—and you agreed—that a little more sleep and considerably less junk food would probably be a good idea. You resolved to take positive action— which you immediately did.

It was also at that point, Julie, that I changed Amanda's name to "Sunshine." She resisted at first, but if you remember, it took only a week or so before she really liked the idea. Today if I forget and call her Amanda Gail, she quickly corrects me by saying, "My name is 'Sunshine!'"

I don't know and I'm sure you and your mother don't really know what was the determining factor. I have an idea that changing her diet, increasing her sleep, and making her name a positive one all played a part in the change.

I mention this to you, Julie, because there's certainly a lesson for all of us when our child is acting in a manner that is not characteristic. Maybe we should explore. Perhaps it's physical, or even emotional. At any rate, all I know is that the granddaughter I love so much and who had loved me so much had really caused me deep concern when she refused to have anything to do with me. You know, I got POWERFUL unhappy about that. And then came the change. How exciting it was to have her run to me and hug me and kiss me and call me "Grandy" as only she can do! Sure do love you *and* the Sunshine Girl.

Love,

DAD

Thought: *When someone we love is having difficulty and is giving us a bad time, it's better to explore the cause than to criticize the action.*

EVERYBODY'S HURTING SOMEWHERE

Dear Family and everybody else,

One of the most exciting things I do in life is to help teach the four-day "Born to Win" Seminar here in Dallas. Two years ago I had one of those never-to-be-forgotten experiences that really opened my eyes and taught me a beautiful lesson.

The class consisted of people from all walks of life. At the end of the four days, had you asked me to select a particular class member who had "put it all together," I would have immediately selected a beautiful black girl from Chicago. She was a beauty queen, and a quick glance would tell you why she was chosen. She looked like a queen, walked like a queen, talked like a queen, and acted like a queen. She was about twenty-four years old, had a beautiful speaking voice which was strong and clear and could be heard with bell-like clarity in a large room. Yet it was totally feminine. She was a college graduate, very articulate, and was in business for herself with over a hundred employees. She was of high moral character and, as I say, seemed to have it all together.

When I finished my talk Saturday afternoon and dismissed the class, she asked me if I would talk to her privately for a few minutes. Of course I agreed, and we moved out of hearing range of the other class members and sat down. She looked at me and said, "Today I found out why I came from Chicago to attend this class. Your last talk was aimed at me." Then she started to lose her composure and tears filled her eyes. She paused for a moment, and then continued. "You're the first person who ever looked at me and told me that I was important, that I was somebody, that I was unique, that I could accomplish objectives in life. I just want you to know that I am deeply grateful for your caring." And then she broke down.

As I say, the experience was an eye-opener, and the lesson is so important I don't want you to miss it. I resolved that day that in the future when I'm dealing with a fellow human being, I will assume that he is hurting and deal with him accordingly. I will assume that a word of encouragement will not be misplaced, and that it will help the recipient to move more easily along life's highways. I hope you will deal with our fellow human beings in a similar manner.

Love,

DAD

Thought: *Sometimes appearances are deceiving. In your relationships with others, if you assume the other person is hurting and deal with that person accordingly, you will be right in most cases. Even when you are wrong, and the other person is not hurting, you will still be right in treating him or her gently.*

LAUGHTER

Dear Sweetnin' and everyone else,

I'm sitting in my little "crow's nest," just outside my office at "Sugarville," our home at Holly Lake. I just heard your beautiful laugh, as it escaped out the kitchen door and made its way up to my spot. Since I'm writing the "Family" book at this moment, I thought it only appropriate that I comment on one of the most beautiful sounds in the world, which is the sound of those I love who are laughing. You do have a beautiful laugh, Cindy, as do your little brother and your two sisters. To be honest, however, none of you laugh *quite* like your mother, whose laughter has a musical happiness that makes it, for me, the most excitingly beautiful sound in the world.

The marvelous thing about all my family's laughter is the depth and happiness of that laughter. All the laughs seem to come from deep inside the heart and soul. Even more beautiful is the fact that the laughter is always either with joy and gladness or a sharing laughter when you are thrilled that something delightful or humorous has happened. You don't laugh *at* others. You always laugh *with* them.

Actually, Cindy, all of us have a lot to laugh about. I'm convinced that anyone who enjoys reasonably good health, lives in America, comes from a loving family, and knows Jesus Christ as Lord has a lot to laugh about. I'm also convinced that if all Americans took serious inventory and compared their situations to those of people who live in other countries, they would realize just how much they have to be grateful for and to laugh about!

Love,

DAD

Love Is 43

It's True: *Laugh and the world laughs with you; cry and you cry alone.*

LOVING YOUR GRANDCHILDREN SURELY IS FUN

Dear Keeper and everybody else,

It'll be several years before you read this, but I've got an idea that when you get a little older your mother and dad will read it to you, and then later you will read it yourself. Right now we're just having a hilarious time with you as our granddaughter. You're beginning to move around pretty well, Keeper, and each day you move faster and further.

At the moment our little game is "I'm gonna get you!" and when I clap my hands and say, "I'm gonna get you," you take off running as fast as you can with me in hot pursuit. By the time you get old enough to read and understand this, Keeper, you will know that I could have caught you in one step, but that would have ended the fun, wouldn't it? So, around and around I chase you, and then I catch you. I pick you up and kiss you and play with you. I put words in your mouth and talk to you and just have a ball!

Through it all, Keeper, I'm praising God that He sent you our way. Sure do love you, Keeper!

YOUR GRANDDADDY

Thought: *Chasing a fifteen-month-old will keep you*

*young and active. Spending that time with
her lays a solid foundation for a loving lifetime relationship.*

"TERRIFIC TWOS"
WILL PRODUCE
"TREMENDOUS THREES"

Dear Sunshine,

I'll never forget the day I walked in from an out-of-town trip and you were on the opposite side of the den with your mother. You looked up and shouted, "There's Grandy!" I watched you as you ran to me and couldn't help but notice that beautiful, long, blonde hair for which any shampoo company in the world would be smart to claim credit; those bright blue eyes which will break hearts for years to come; a personality the likes of which has never been seen on television; and an intelligence which Einstein himself would have envied! (I'm confident you parents and grandparents greatly admire my forthright presentation of the unbiased facts as they relate to my granddaughter.) I picked you up and you hugged me, gave me a big kiss, reared back, looked me straight in the eye, and said, "Love my Grandy!"

I can't imagine anyone with the audacity to refer to such a gorgeous little girl as one of the "Terrible Twos." You were two years old at the time, and you were a "Terrific Two." Later you became a "Tremendous Three," then a "Fantastic Four," a "Fabulous Five," a "Super Six." Now you are a "Sensational Seven" and well on your way to becoming a "Great Eight."

Watching you go through those formative years has been exciting and rewarding. I know that if all of us continue to think in those positive terms about each year in your life you will have a much better chance in life. The Bible does say "As ye sow, so also shall ye reap."

Love,

GRANDY

P.S. *I'm glad you love me, Sunshine, because I sure do love you!*

Fact: *Identify those special years as "Terrific Twos" and you will have "Tremendous Threes" and so on. Identify them as the "Terrible Twos" and you will have the "Trying Threes." It's up to you, but remember that the choice you make as a parent could make the difference in what your child does with his life.*

LOVE IS FOR MOUNTAINTOPS *AND* VALLEYS

Dear Sugar Babe,

Tonight was one of those nights at the church. God's Spirit was working as I've seldom seen it work. The men on the staff did a beautiful job as they opened with what could have been a comedy, but turned into beautiful, spirit-filled music. Then

Barbara Law sang, as only she can, that great song, "Peace in My Soul." I just naturally feel a little closer to Heaven when she raises her magnificent voice in song.

The pastor was especially moving and effective tonight as he talked about the shed blood of our Lord, and the Lord's Supper itself seemed to have a very special significance. Through it all I was so grateful for you. As I've told you so many times, when I'm having either a mountaintop or a valley experience, I especially want you with me. Just being able to hold your hand is one of the things I enjoy tremendously. This makes me know how much you are a part of everything I do. I enjoy being with you all the time, but especially on occasions like tonight.

As you know, when I'm out of town I never go sightseeing and seldom accept lengthy dinner engagements unless you are along. I don't really enjoy spending two or three hours in a beautiful place unless you're there to share it. I guess all of that adds up to the fact that for a long time, Sweetheart, I've had quite a case as far as you're concerned, and it seems to be getting worse—or let's make that "better"—as the years go by.

Not too long ago somebody asked me what I do for entertainment, and I said, "I married her." Actually, I married far more than entertainment. I married excitement, peace, love, and a lifestyle that is so perfectly adapted to me.

As much as I love you on those "mountaintop" experiences, I honestly feel that I love you even more during a "valley" experience. I don't have many valley experiences, but when I do I want you with me. In the last few years these experiences have almost always occurred when I am tired and worn out. During those times, as you know, I don't want much conversation. I do want lots of quiet, hugging affection time. It's during those times that my need for you and your support of me give so much meaning to my life. I'm convinced that any real love story involves the filling of deep needs, and you certainly meet all my needs, whether they involve sharing the mountaintop or helping me climb out of the valley.

Your ever-lovin',

ZIG

> P.S. *In many ways life and marriage are both roller coaster affairs with a certain number of highs and lows. The beautiful thing about sharing life and marriage with you, Sweetheart, is that you make the mountaintop more exhilarating and the valleys more bearable.*

WILL GOD REALLY "PLAY" WITH US?

Dear Sunshine and everybody else,

My goodness, what a child has been taught really does show up early! The day after you were five years old your mother was busy, your grandparents were not around, and your friends were all gone. Your mother was explaining that you would have to play alone and your response to that was, "No, I'm not alone. God will play with me."

Now some people might think that was a little impertinent or even sacrilegious, but your mom and your grandparents instantly knew what you were saying. From birth you have been told that God is with you at all times. Since your friends could not be with you, it just made sense that if God was with you He might as well play with you.

Theologically I'm not certain that God will play with you,

but I certainly would not challenge that statement because God is interested in the happiness of all of His children. And you certainly are one of His. About the only thing God can't do, Sunshine, is have grandchildren, because all of us are His sons and daughters. I'm pleased that God permitted me to be a grandfather, especially since He gave me a granddaughter like you.

Love,

GRANDY

ONE GOOD WAY TO KEEP YOUR MATE LOVING YOU

I like: *love* Zig

Because: He's absolutely the best husband ever! He shares his love for me not only with me, but with other people. I never have to wonder - I know. He takes good care of me and is kind and considerate. He has influenced (with God's help) so many people and I'm so proud of him - I thank God for him and will try to be a better, more loving and understanding wife. In case he's wondering - I love him - all the way!

S B

Note: *These little "I like because" slips can be used to communicate your love to your mate, to encourage your children, to motivate your employees and fellow workers, or to inspire anyone to do a better job. When these slips are sincerely used they can give the recipient and the writer a tremendous lift.*

P.S. *When I get one of these goodies from the Redhead, it sure makes my day!*

LIFE *IS* UNCERTAIN

Dear Sweetnin' and everybody else's children,

I'm sure you remember the first car that was exclusively yours and brand new. It was a Volkswagen and my, how you could whip that little car around and how much you enjoyed it! But then one day you were involved in an accident and taken to the hospital.

I was assured that you were all right and there were no serious problems. However, when I walked into the emergency room and saw you, I could not contain myself. Many thoughts and emotions flooded my mind. The fact that you were apparently all right was comforting, but the fear of hidden injuries was also in my mind.

In a matter of seconds I replayed countless phases of your life. I thought of the joy of your arrival and the uniqueness of your birth announcement. The tiny nurse had come out and told me that we had a little boy and that you and your mother were fine. I had your grandmother Abernathy on the phone when that same little nurse came rushing out and said, "No, it's a girl!" I laughingly told her that there was a difference. I thought about the joy of watching you grow and the excitement of seeing you go through the phases of childhood. These and many other thoughts flooded my mind.

Then there was that accident, and I stood there with the full realization that life truly is uncertain. It crossed my mind that had you been going slightly faster, or if circumstances had been mildly different, the life of my beautiful daughter whom I love so much could have been lost. All of these thoughts were in my mind, but when I saw that you really were all right the overwhelming feeling of relief overcame me and the tears of joy gushed forth. Of course, you didn't help a bit because you blubbered about as badly as your dad. I suppose what that really says, Sweetnin', is that we love each other.

Love,

DAD

Thought: *If you love somebody, tell them today. You might not have them tomorrow.*

LOVE IS . . . A HUG

Dear Sugar Baby,

On occasion all of us seem to be unaware of the impact we can have on a person with some little act of kindness and/or friendliness. The letter you received from Tammy Johnson, who attended one of our "Born to Win" seminars, is a classic example of what I'm talking about. When she returned from the four-day experience, she wrote you the following note:

Dear Mrs. Ziglar:

You might not know this but you have *changed* my life! Before I met you I was a warm, happy, excited, reserved person. I never hugged anyone but those very, very close to me. I am unable to have children, and, believe it or not, I didn't even hug kids, and stiffly kissed babies. But now I am a warm, happy, excited *HUGGER!*

You showed me how. It's only been a week since I changed, but I feel like a *whole*, new person. Thanks so very much.

The workshop was great! I am renewed!

Love,
Tammy B. Johnson

The thought was beautiful and Tammy expressed it beautifully. To some people a hug is a little thing, but this "little" thing had a significant impact on a life. The message is powerful. When you have love in your heart you are in a position to help others.

I know you were surprised and pleased to learn that you had played such an important part in her life. That's one of the reasons, Sweetheart, I love you as much as I do. Whether you fully realize it or not, you do so many of the "little" things that play an important part in many people's lives.

Your ever-lovin' husband,

ZIG

P.S. *Looks like your reputation as "The Happy Hugger" is well-deserved. As you know, it takes a dozen hugs a day from you for me to survive, twenty if I'm going to get anything done, and thirty if I really want to get in high gear!*

LEARNING TO LOVE
AND CARE FOR OTHERS

Dear Family (and everybody else),

We recently had quite an experience in our four-day "Born to Win" seminar. In this class we had a businessman from Malaysia, a saleslady from Australia, a horticulturist from East Tennessee, and a young man from Dallas. We had many others, but these four were the main characters in a drama that affected the whole class.

Our seminar involves a considerable amount of class participation. From time to time various class members will share personal experiences or lessons they have learned. As each person shares an experience, the other class members write on a slip of paper the good qualities of the presenter and what he likes about the presentation. We call them "I like because" slips (see page 48). The comments might be something like, "I like Joe Jones because he is personable, friendly, sincere, and obviously loves people." When a class member makes three or four presentations he ends up at the end of the week with a handful of "I like because" slips. He uses them as boosters for months after the class. Each class member also develops the ability to find the good in other people. Response and results have been absolutely magnificent.

The horticulturist was bright and successful in his profession but could neither read nor write. His wife had shared that information with us earlier, so we had arranged assignments to make certain he shared only personal experiences with us.

On the third day he stood up to make his presentation and started by saying, "I want all of you to know how much I have appreciated the 'I like because' slips. They give me more encouragement than anything I've ever received, and I love all of you for them. I wish so much that I could write you some 'I like because' slips, but I can't." At this point he broke down, but then continued, "You see, I can neither read nor write, and my wife has been reading to me all of the good things you've been writing about me."

Again, he broke down and when he did the business executive from Malaysia, the saleslady from Australia, and the young man from Dallas all jumped up simultaneously, ran to the front of the class, threw their arms around him, and they all cried like babies. When this happened, a spontaneous standing ovation from the entire class occurred. There was not a dry eye in the room.

As this scene took place, I thought to myself, "How tragic that the United Nations is not here to see what is taking place." These four seemed to represent all of mankind: three different faiths, both sexes, three different countries, and a tremendous range of intellectual and business accomplishment. Yet, they truly loved and cared for each other after they came to know one another.

Love,

DAD

Lesson: *It has been said that a stranger is a friend we haven't met, and I believe that is at least partially true. I also believe you can live with someone many years and still be strangers. You don't necessarily come to know a person just by living with him. You know people by sharing your thoughts, dreams, plans, hopes, ambitions and experiences. You know people by talking with them and writing to them. You know people by looking at them and studying them. You love and respect them*

when you learn to identify their good quali-
ties and tell them about these good, positive
qualities. The more good you see and com-
pliment, the more good there will be to see
and compliment.

LIFE IS EXCITING . . .
AND LOVE IS LISTENING

Dear Tom (and all other "turned on" sons and daughters),

I don't believe I've ever seen you any more cranked up than you were last night! When you came in from the church basketball game you were wide-open, full-speed ahead. Even though your team had lost the game, your enthusiasm was absolutely incredible. You had had a good time associating with good people, and you were part of a team — and that's good.

In retrospect, it's too bad we didn't have a recorder going during the entire conversation. As you recall, when you got home your mother and I had been watching the news when I was interrupted by a phone call from a friend. We chatted for probably ten minutes, after which I got up to go back to pack for my trip. As I started to leave, you looked at me, smiled, and said, "Sit a minute, Dad." So I sat down. You proceeded to tell me all about the events of the evening. Then you told me how excited you were about what you were learning in school, especially from your Bible teacher who was so fantastic. You told me how he had taken the Book of Acts and made it live so vividly that it seemed like a novel instead of a book out of the Bible.

Next, Son, you told me about the plans you had for coaching the first-graders in physical education during one of the study halls you have this year. Then you told me about how you and a friend were planning to start a discipleship class for freshmen. You planned to take seven or eight of the guys and share with them the things you've been learning about the Bible.

By then it was getting late and I said, "Son, I've got to pack for tomorrow before it gets too late." That didn't discourage you in the least. You simply got up and walked back with me, and while I was packing you were going non-stop. I had to go back into my office a couple of times and into the den once, but you were with me every step of the way, chattering like a magpie. I finished packing and brushing my teeth in step with your conversation.

Of course I was responding because I was truly interested and excited about what you were saying. Finally I just had to say, "Son, I'm delighted to see you so excited, but I've got to get up at six tomorrow morning and I have a tough two-day road trip. We've got to go to bed." You laughed good-naturedly and said, "O.K., Dad, but I doubt that I'm going to be able to go to sleep I'm so cranked up!"

All in all we had quite an evening. I was excited, too, Son, maybe because of your excitement and the fact that we had communicated freely and openly.

Love,

DAD

Thought: *Pay close attention to what your children say. Keep the lines of communication open. They want to — need to — and will talk to somebody. What better person than you, the parent who loves them?*

IF YOU
LOVE 'EM,
TELL 'EM

Dear Tom and everybody else,

Had you been a few years older I would have accused you of being a manipulator, but at age four I naturally believe there was no guile in your heart. You really got next to me, Son. You probably won't remember it, so let me re-create the scene.

Mom and Dad had just bought you a tricycle—unassembled (serious mistake). You're eighteen years old now, Son, and you know Dad's intense dislike for doing *anything* of a mechanical nature beyond screwing in a lightbulb. Not only do I not like it, but, realistically, I'm all thumbs and a little short of patience when things don't go together.

In the case of the tricycle, I was really struggling. I had just put some of the parts together, but I had gotten them backwards. With some exasperation I was muttering under my breath and sweat was popping out on my brow and through my shirt. You were sitting quietly, hopefully, expectantly. At the precise moment I was about to abandon the project—at least temporarily—you looked straight at me and said, "I sure do love you, Dad." Well, needless to say, old Dad stuck around and finished assembling that tricycle.

I've thought about the magic of the words "I love you" many times since that incident. How marvelous life would be if we could just teach the men and women of the world the importance of truly caring for each other, and then expressing that care with those three beautiful words. If that happened, there would be many, many more people who not only would put tricycles together but would put their lives together in a far more meaningful way.

Love,

DAD

Fact: *Genuine expressions of love motivate us to do even more for those we love.*

210-POUND MAN VS. A 6-OUNCE CHIPMUNK

Dear Julie and all other children with loving fathers,

I don't know how, but I had largely forgotten the incident until you brought it up over the weekend. I'm talking about the day your chipmunk got out and was running all over the back yard at our home in Columbia, South Carolina. Somehow, and to this day I don't know exactly how, I managed to run him down and pick him up.

The next two minutes had to be the most painful two minutes of my life. There I was, a two-hundred-pounder chasing a 6-ounce chipmunk all over the yard, and finally having caught it, was now desperately wanting to get rid of him! That little varmint had bitten through the fleshy part of the end of one of my fingers and was holding on for dear life! Blood was gushing all over the place. What I really wanted to do was throw that chipmunk down and use what little meat there was as dogfood or maybe even hamburger meat. In short, I wanted to get rid of that animal—instantly!

Then I looked into your face. Those eyes and that expression melted my heart. Without uttering a word you told me how much you loved me, but at the same time you were telling me that you loved that little chipmunk and "if there is *anything* you can do, Daddy, to save my chipmunk, oh, that would be just marvelous, Daddy!" Yet you also seemed to be saying, "If you can't, I'll understand. But I hope you can, Daddy, and I believe you can."

Needless to say, I did hold on, and I did manage to put the little critter in a cereal box. By the time some of that pain had subsided, I actually thought it was funny. Two days later when the finger started swelling and turning black, the shot the doctor gave me reminded me of the painful experience. But I say it again, the look in your eyes and your expressions were payment in full for the few minutes of grief and pain I underwent. Actually, considering everything, that little chipmunk was fun to have around! Sure do love you, Little One.

DAD

Thought: *I hope this doesn't sound like I'm trying to sound like I'm a sacrificial lamb. I hope it does communicate that I'm firmly convinced that if you really do love someone you will be willing to undergo pain for that person. Incidentally, for fear you might miss the point, the big winner in this event was old Dad.*

LIFE'S LITTLE COINCIDENCES

Dear Sweetnin',

There's nothing more exciting or pleasing to your old dad

than to talk to one of his very own who's excited and happy and who tells old Dad some of the good things he likes to hear. What a thrill for you to tell me that when you and your brother went camping during the week he spent with you that he seemed to have all of the answers to the Biblical questions you asked.

Even more exciting was the fact that you were so enthusiastic about his Christian spirit and his willingness to share with you. It was also exciting when one of your co-workers quit and you had a chance to work her hours which freed you on Sunday morning so you could go to church. What a thrill when you were asked why you wanted Sunday morning off to have you respond that you wanted to go to church. By "coincidence," a lady standing close by was able to recommend the very church about which your mother and I had heard so many good things. Yes, Sweetnin', God does work in mysterious ways. Sure do love you, Baby!

DAD

P.S. *Since God knows our needs even before we express them, I know you know that it wasn't a "coincidence" that the lady was standing close by to direct you to the right church.*

Fact: *When you are tuned in to God's will, He will find a way.*

Question: *What is love?*
Answer: *God*

KIDS GIVE THEIR DADS THE DARNDEST THINGS!

Dear Julie,

As you well know, our family has long held the very firm opinion that Dad is a tough guy to buy for, and I would have to agree. God has been so good to us that He's certainly given me far more than I need, and I have very few wants in life. The net result is that when you and your brother and sisters ask me what I want for special occasions from Christmas to Father's Day I have a standard reply: "Just give me a frozen watermelon."

Obviously, I never expected to get a frozen watermelon, so when you came lugging one in on one of those special occasions, I was both delighted and surprised. I thought to myself, "Who else in the world would have done such a thing but my "Little One," the girl who consistently does the unexpected?"

Love,

DAD

> Thought: *Be careful what you ask for because whether it's silly or serious, good for you or bad, the chances are good that if you keep asking you will get it.*

THE APPRECIATED GRADUATION GIFT

Dear Suzie and all other children,

I'm certain you remember the occasion. You were fresh from graduation night at Dreher High School in Columbia, South Carolina. At that particular moment, Dad was on a "winning streak," and I had promised to buy you a car. I found one in Atlanta, Georgia, exactly like you wanted. It was a GTO Pontiac, which was the "in" car for teenagers at the time. I finished a meeting in Atlanta after midnight and headed for home. As you know, Doll, I have a tendency to get sleepy on long road trips, and I was particularly tired on this occasion. Between roadside naps I probably fought sleep as hard as I've ever fought it in my life as I drove the two hundred-plus miles from Atlanta to Columbia.

As I pulled into the driveway at roughly 5:45 A.M., who should I see but my beautiful teenage daughter, jumping up and down, clapping her hands, squealing, shouting, and going through all the gyrations that only an ecstatic teenager can do. When I stepped out of the car and you hugged me and kissed me a couple of dozen times between your declarations of love and affection, my eyes opened wide and all thoughts of sleep and tiredness just disappeared.

Isn't it amazing, Doll, what love and appreciation can do for us? Isn't it a shame that all of us don't show the love and appreciation we often feel but are reluctant to reveal? Sure do love you, Doll.

DAD

Thought: *The attitude of gratitude is truly beautiful.*
Express it often, and the chances are good

*your eyes will be opened to more things to
be grateful for.*

TOUGH LOVE

Dear Parent,

Do you love your eighteen-year-old enough to kick him
or her out of the house? That sounds like a challenging,
intriguing—even contradictory—question, but here's what I
have in mind. Dr. Forest Tennant of the University of California at Los Angeles is perhaps the number one drug authority
in America. He regularly works with two thousand drug
addicts in his clinics and has documented more evidence
concerning the effects of drugs and the treatment for drug
abuse than anyone else in our society.

Dr. Tennant says that if a youngster is involved in drugs,
when he reaches age eighteen you give him the option of
getting off drugs or becoming 100 percent self-supporting. If
he refuses to give up the drugs and if you truly love him and
want to help him, you will definitely kick him out of the
house. Dr. Tennant contends that if you support your child at
home, you are simply supporting the habit, and his chances
of freeing himself of drugs are virtually non-existent. He
goes so far as to say he cannot document a single case where
the youngster over eighteen stayed at home and managed to
kick the habit.

On the "kick out" side, Dr. Tennant cannot recall a single
instance where the parents forced their eighteen-year-old son
or daughter to leave and become self-supporting that they
did not eventually come back home drug free or willing to
enter treatment to become drug free. Without exception,

these young people report that forcing them to accept responsibility for their behavior was the greatest thing that ever happened to them.

It would be sheer speculation on my part if I should attempt to give reasons for this, but in my judgment there are several things to be considered. Number one, when the youngster sees that the parents are adamant in their opposition to drugs and are absolutely determined not to support the child's drug habit by supporting the child, they realize their problem is serious and that they are responsible for solving the problem.

Number two, there is a possibility the child really does seek parental approval and is getting anything but that approval by the use of drugs. Perhaps they realize that when they are in the real world and have to support themselves they cannot do so with a mind that is "fouled up" with drugs.

Whatever the reason, I repeat, Dr. Tennant has documented outstanding success in getting youngsters off drugs if parents refuse to support the habit and turn them out of the house. By the same token, parents have experienced almost complete failure when the youngster is supported at home by the parents.

It really boils down to this, parents: Do you love your child enough to make that painful decision to send him or her off where they will have a chance to escape the terribly destructive drug habit? It'll be a tough decision, but if you're ever faced with the problem, the choice you make will be a direct indication as to how deeply you love your child, and not what you fear "others" will think. Give it some thought.

ZIG ZIGLAR

Note: *The youngster under eighteen is a different story. You seek help and maintain support of the younger child. The book,* Tough Love,

*by Phyllis and David York, will be helpful.
Write for more information to Community
Service Foundation, Box 70, Sellersville, Penn-
sylvania 18960.*

Lesson: *Real love is best demonstrated when you do
for the child what is best for the child. This
is not always what you want to do, but it is
always what you should do.*

LOVE YOUR MATE—
AND LET THE
CHILDREN KNOW IT

Dear Cindy,

Thanks for your letter of August 22. It's always nice to hear
from "the Sweetnin'."

Amazing, isn't it, how we parents—and for that matter,
children—sometimes take so many things for granted. You
said some neat things in that letter, but one thing that stood
out was your expression of gratitude for the love I have for
all of you, especially your mom.

In many ways each of your sisters and your brother have
expressed the same thing, but your letter really hit me as to
how critically important it is for parents to love each other
and to demonstrate that love. This gives children a sense of
security because they know that since mom and dad truly
love each other, they will work out their differences. They do
this for their own benefit and enjoyment, but also so their

children can grow up in a loving, stable atmosphere. Of course, I'm doubly fortunate, because your mother is so easy to love that loving her just came naturally! *Showing* that love and never taking her for granted requires thought and vigilance, as well as an occasional reminder from "the Sweetnin'."

Love,

DAD

I Believe: *The best way to make your wife and children feel secure is not with big deposits in bank accounts, but with little deposits of thoughtfulness and affection in the "love account."*

IF YOU LOVE THEM, TELL THEM NOW

Dear Suzie and all small children,

As you know, your mother and dad had some pretty old-fashioned ideas about raising you, your sisters, and your brother. We wanted to know where you were at all times and what you were doing. We had strict ideas concerning your safety around water, high places, and the street. We set down some strict guidelines to go by, and that meant each of you were to stay out of the street at all times. One day in Florence, South Carolina, when you were about two years old, we suddenly missed you. I ran out front looking for you, and then I dashed down the street, but you were nowhere to be seen. When I looked back in the other direction, there you were, more than a block away across a busy, busy highway.

I made a mad dash to my car, took off as fast as the car would go, slammed on the brakes, hopped out and got my little girl. Suzan, since you are now a mother yourself, you know that sometimes parents punish their children for disobedience. On occasion I have taken that route. However, that day there was no punishment. There was a big bucket of tears of gratitude that God had sent His guardian angel down to hold my little girl's hand as she walked across an extremely busy highway.

Wouldn't it be great, Doll, if everyone took more time expressing love and gratitude for each other, for God's goodness, and for the blessings and mercy which we all receive? How sad that it often takes a crisis, an illness, or a tragic or near-tragic accident to draw families and loved ones close enough together to show and tell each other of the love and appreciation they feel!

Sure do love you, Doll.

DAD

Resolution: *To find and use opportunities on a regular basis to tell those I love that I do love and appreciate them. After all, I might not have the opportunity tomorrow, and "I wish I had" are among the saddest words most of us will ever utter.*

THE UNIQUE YOU

Dear Little One and all other dessert lovers,

Many things are completely unpredictable, but as a little girl growing up, what you would do when you got to the end of a cafeteria line was always 100 percent predictable. Your mother and I, as well as your two big sisters, knew that you would select the prettiest dessert (this simply means the one with the most color). If there was a piece of cake with any green or pink in it, we knew you would automatically grab that piece for dessert.

Many things, of course, are not predictable because life itself is so unpredictable. But your dessert selection procedure was unique and special to all of us. It provided us with many light moments to know what our "Little One" was going to do when she got to the end of the line and dessert-picking time came along. Just a small thing, Little One, but it was one of those incidents that made you such a very special little girl to us. Sure do love you, Baby.

DAD

Thought: *Over ten billion people have walked the earth since the beginning of time, and every last one of them,* including you, *is unique and different in countless ways, including the way we look and perhaps even the dessert we select.*

IF YOU LOVE THEM, PLAY SHOW AND TELL

Dear Cindy (and all other members of any family),

Sometimes it's absolutely amazing the lengths to which some children will go to tell their dad they love him. There are a lot of ways to say a lot of things, but when I learned you had taken up jogging just so you could jog with me the two or three times each year we get together when I speak in San Jose, I was absolutely overwhelmed. Of course, Sweetnin', old Dad believes it's extremely good for you to be a jogger, but to run twelve months out of the year so that you can jog a few times during the year with me certainly has got to rate as a real sacrifice.

If more parents and children went out of their way to do things to show their love and affection for each other, the world would be a much better place to live. Sure do love you, Sweetnin'.

DAD

Thought: *Love can be expressed in a thousand different ways, but it should be expressed in at least one way (word, deed, or action) every day to family members you see on a daily basis and regularly to family members you do not see often. Out of sight should not mean out of mind.*

IT'S GOOD
TO HAVE
GRANDPARENTS
CLOSE BY

Dear Sunshine and all other four-year-olds,

You are at age four which, in your case, is the "verification" stage of your life. You are Grandy's jogging buddy and I love it! Generally speaking, we start enthusiastically, but after we've run about a hundred steps you decide to walk. That's where the fun starts.

Almost always you will say, "Grandy, we need to stay on the side of the street, right?" And of course, I completely agree by replying "Right!" Then you will say, "Because some cars might come along and hit us, right?" And again I verify it with a "Right!" All the way around the block you seek that reassurance from me that it is "right." As a general rule, for a good portion of our trip you develop certain little problems that necessitate my carrying you. That's not all bad, because when I'm carrying you I can talk to you better and get lots of kisses.

I'll tell you for sure, God was "right" when He gave me a "Sunshine" girl. He was also right when He gave you grandparents. Bill Gothard, in his seminars on Basic Youth Conflicts, stresses the advantages that children have when they live close to their grandparents. It gives the family stability, continuity, support, and love by providing grandchildren two more loving adult role models with which to identify. It also offers grandparents a closer on-going relationship not only with the grandchildren but with their own children as well. Those are mighty important things, Sunshine, and you sure are important to us.

Love,

GRANDY

Fact: *Love is — or can be — children and grandchildren.*

A WELCOME LETTER FROM A MUCH-LOVED DAUGHTER

June, 1981

Dear Daddy,

To me it seems like my real relationship with you only began about five years ago. I loved you before then and I missed you when you were out of town. I was always happy when you were home but I can't remember us really knowing each other.

I remember best the three spankings you loved me enough to give me as I was growing up, and the times you went to my horse shows. Oh, yes, and the time I lost the tennis match at the fairgrounds. I wanted to win that one for you. I felt that day like I felt later when my horse, Irish, wouldn't jump. I wanted you to be so proud of me.

That's how I feel today. I want to be a success — I want people to say, "That's Julie Ziglar, Zig Ziglar's daughter. She's real successful in business and one of the best speakers anywhere." I've always wanted to be like you. I've been afraid to tell you because I wasn't sure I could ever be as great as you, and I don't want to let you down. I think now that if I keep on doing what I'm doing everything will fall into place.

I got off the subject. What I really want to say is that I'm so proud to have you as a father. I want to get to know you better. You hardly ever talk about yourself. What makes you do things the way you do? Where does all of that drive come from? It was there long before you came to know Christ. How did you know to go after a speaking career? I think I could write a good book, but when does a person know if he or she really has something worth saying?

Oh, Daddy, there is so much to know and time seems so short. Sometimes I want a husband and sometimes I don't. Every time I meet somebody that I think might be the one I get so wrapped up in the relationship that I take my eyes off of my business goals. I'm even getting to the point where I feel the hassle to meet someone new interrupts my whole life. I don't want to be selfish, but when will I know what to do?

I want us to get together and just talk some, but I want to talk about you. I think if I can learn about you, I'll know more about me.

It's time for bed now. Tomorrow is another full day. Business is really booming just now. Say a prayer for me. God and I still have a lot of work to do to achieve the kind of person we want me to be.

With all of my very best love,

JULIE

I love you Daddy.

Dear Little One,

What a beautiful letter! As your little (now big) brother said so often when he was five or six years old, "That makes me feel good." It's exciting to know that things are going well for you, but that's not surprising because you are a very determined young woman. Naturally, I'm pleased that you want to be a great speaker because it's gratifying when one you love approves of the profession you have chosen. My observation, Little One, as a speech course instructor and not as a proud poppa, is that you have everything needed to be a truly outstanding speaker—good voice, good platform presence, outstanding attractiveness and charisma, great enthusiasm, and valid subject matter. All you need is time and experience, and you've got plenty of time for that.

On the "disappointment" bit, let me assure you that, yes, I was "disappointed" when Irish wouldn't jump, and I was "disappointed" when you lost the tennis match. However, my disappointment had little to do with what I wanted for me and much to do with what I wanted for you.

Just remember that I'll never feel that you have let me down when you do your best, and you always do that. You're a winner, Little One, and as a proud and loving dad I look forward to getting to know you better and better. I'm obviously pleased that you want to learn more about what makes old Dad tick!

Love,

DAD

P.S. from Dad: Julie is now happily married to Jim Norman, a fine Christian man.

LOVING *ALL*
YOUR CHILDREN

Dear Cindy and all other non-first-born children,

I don't know if you ever really knew this or not, but before you made your appearance I was honestly worried about my ability to love you as totally and completely as I loved your big sister. You see, Sweetnin', I loved her so much and felt she was unique, beautiful, bright, and different. I could not visualize loving another child as I did Suzan. I did not realize that each child is totally different, special and unique, so I truly was worried about loving you in the way I loved your big sister.

I gotta confess, Sweetnin', that feeling lasted for nearly sixty seconds after you made your entrance into the world and into my arms. When we learned that Julie and, later, Tom, were on the way, I never gave a thought to whether I would love them as I did you and Suzan. I had learned my lesson!

There are lots of miracles in our world, but none can compare to the birth of a beautiful baby. It's magnificent! When I look at you, your sisters, your brother, your mother, and my two granddaughters and realize your uniqueness, I'm always amazed to encounter people who actually believe that we got our start as globs of protoplasm. Incredible! Anyhow, I just wanted you to know that I truly do love you, that you are unique, that you are different, and, best of all, God trusted us with you.

Love,

DAD

Fact: *Some ten billion-plus people have walked the earth but there is not now nor has there ever been another one like you.*

Love Is: *A baby.*

WITH PAIN THERE
IS OFTEN GAIN

Dear Family (and everybody else),

The casual observer who looks at my life today could come to the conclusion that my life is not all that tough. They would be at least partially right because compared to what my schedule was like for a long while, it certainly is considerably easier. That doesn't mean I'm not working as hard, because in many ways I am working harder than ever before. I don't have some of the problems and obstacles I had a few years ago, however, and that's what I want to talk about.

In the last thirty years, society has raised millions of our citizens to believe that if it doesn't look good, smell good, taste good, and isn't fun, we should have nothing to do with it. That's a tragic state of affairs because one of the things I constantly assert—because I believe it so strongly—is that life is not easy. Life is tough, regardless of whether you're a doctor, household executive, traveling salesman, attorney, schoolteacher, serviceman, secretary, minister, or even public speaker.

Yes, I believe that life is tough, but this I know: If you're tough on yourself, life is going to be infinitely easier on you. I believe that today, as never before, life is enormously exciting and tremendously rewarding, but that doesn't mean it's easy. It does mean that on many occasions you're going to have to "suck it up and tough it out" and simply hang in there.

There'll be many days when you don't really feel like going to work, but a sense of responsibility, discipline, and commitment will drag you out of bed, and you'll be on your way to do what you were hired to do. You accepted that responsibility when you accepted the job. Interestingly enough, once you get into the physical process of doing something, chances are superb that you will feel like doing it.

All of you, with the exception of Keeper and Sunshine, are old enough to know that I'm not bragging when I say that I exercise a certain amount of discipline and commitment myself, so I'm not preaching something I haven't practiced. As you know, on December 13, 1982, I went to the Cooper Clinic for my annual physical. While there I stayed on the treadmill longer than any member of the Dallas Cowboys football team. My resting heartbeat registered forty, and I can physically do things I could not do when I was twenty-five years old. I can outrun 98 percent of the college kids in America on a five-mile run, which means either that I'm in pretty good shape or most of the college kids are in terrible shape. I suspect it's a little of both.

When I finish my bragging, Dr. Cooper, who is now a close, personal friend, smiles and says, "Yeah, Zig, that's pretty good. But let me tell you about a sixty-five-year-old lady who lives here in Dallas. She started jogging when she was fifty-nine and has just completed her tenth marathon. Two of them were fifty miles long." When I pick myself up off the deck, Dr. Cooper then tells me about the fifteen-year-old sophomore girl at Trinity Christian Academy who also did a great deal better on the treadmill than I did.

Actually, family, I'm not bragging on old Dad, nor am I bragging on the sixty-five-year-old lady or the fifteen-year-old girl. What I am saying is that inside each one of you and

our fellow Americans is an incredible amount of potential—
physical, mental, and spiritual. What you do with that potential is up to you.

I give you the details of my physical condition because
eleven years ago when I started my exercise program I could
only run one city block. Until then my idea of exercise had
been to fill the tub, take a bath, pull the plug, and fight the
current. I know you'll agree that is not really much of an
organized exercise program!

For twenty-four years of my adult life—by choice—I weighed
well over two hundred pounds. I say "by choice" because I
have never "accidentally" taken a bite of anything. Every bite
I've eaten has been premeditated. I even set aside three
specific times every day to do nothing but eat!

One other example I use to stress that life isn't easy is the
fact that I made over three thousand speeches before I ever
received a fee. It's true that many of those were sales training
seminars and sales meetings I conducted for my own organi-
zation. A number of them were to groups when I was selling
tickets to hear other speakers, so I did receive some remunera-
tion. There were many, many occasions, however, when I
drove as far as two hundred miles at night one way, at my own
expense, to speak to fifteen or twenty people. Then I would
drive back that night so I could go to work the next day. I was
willing to do this because I honestly felt that I had something
to say and that the day would come when my efforts would be
rewarded.

I was obsessed with the idea that this was what I wanted to
do with my life. I also knew that in order to reap those
rewards I would have to hone and polish my skills until they
were professional.

I do not believe now, nor have I ever believed, that we do
our young people a service when we delude them into believing that life is a bowl of cherries, that it's easy. Life isn't easy.
Life is tough.

I'm completely convinced that parents who truly love their children will teach them by word and example that if they are tough on themselves, then life will be much easier on them. This approach will also let them see that life can be beautiful, fun, exciting, and rewarding *if* we are tough — tough on ourselves. With children, especially small ones, we often have to be "loving tough" until they mature enough to be tough on themselves.

The way Brother Bern and Sister Elaine Lofchick of Winnipeg, Canada, dealt with their son, David, is a classic example of what I'm talking about. As a two-year-old with cerebral palsy, David had to wear heavy, painful leg braces that needed to be progressively tightened each evening. Night after night David, who was a beautiful little boy, would plead with his mother and dad to leave the braces off, or not to make them so tight, but Bernie and Elaine loved David so much they said "no" to the tears of the moment so they could say "yes" to the laughter of a lifetime. That's love.

All of this simply says, family, that sometimes when the going gets tough and you, or yours, get tired of hanging in there and toughing it out, just remember there is a light at the end of the tunnel. It could well be that when you top the next hill or round the next curve your objective will be in sight. As somebody once said, there is seldom gain without pain, and once you've achieved the gain you forget the pain.

DAD

Fact: *You don't "pay the price" for success, a good marriage, or good health. You "pay the price" for failure, a bad marriage, and poor health. You enjoy the benefits of success, a good marriage, and good health. This doesn't suggest that life is easy, but it does say that when you make a serious, prolonged effort to*

*succeed in your career, your life, and taking
care of your health, the rewards are well
worth the effort.*

A RAY OF LIGHT

Dear Family (and everybody else),

My reputation as a flag-waving, hero-worshipping, family-loving, God-fearing man is pretty well established with you. One of my heroes and good friends is retired Brigadier General Robinson Risner, who has done much to help keep our country strong and free.

I'm sure that on many occasions you've heard the expression, "a ray of light," or "a ray of hope." I personally thought I knew what it meant, but I really didn't until I met "Robbie," who was a prisoner of war in the Vietnam conflict for seven years. Fifty-four months of his confinement were spent in isolation, with ten months in total darkness. Never will I forget my feelings when General Risner shared with me and the Born to Win class an incident during his stay in the "Hanoi Hilton."

As he explained it, when they boarded up his cell, shutting out all light, it was a traumatic experience. He was already under intense physical and mental duress. The years of confinement had taken a toll. His love of God, family, and country had been the glue that had held him together. But now, with not even a glimmer of light, it truly was a traumatic situation.

During this period of time General Risner would get up in the morning and jog in place by the hour. Without this exercise program and constant prayer, he says, he probably would have gone out of his mind. Even with these outlets the pressure was intense, so much so that on occasion he would become so overwrought he would have to scream. General Risner would not give his captors the satisfaction of knowing he was hurting, however, so he stuffed some clothing into his mouth and screamed at the top of his voice.

One morning at daylight, after a particularly frustrating day, General Risner got down on the floor in his seven-by-seven-foot cell and crawled under the bunk where there was a vent in the floor that allowed in fresh air from the outside. He saw a faint glimmer of light reflected on the inside wall of the vent. He put his eye next to the cement wall and discovered a minute crack in the construction to see outside. The hole was so small that all he could see was a single blade of grass. Later he said to me, "Zig, there is no way I can describe to you the joy, the excitement, the gratitude, and the exhilaration I felt when I saw that ray of light and that single blade of grass. It represented life, growth, and freedom, and I knew God had not forgotten me."

I don't know how this strikes you, but that day I made a vow that I would be particularly careful about what I complained about in the future. God bless you, General Risner. Millions of Americans, including me, are grateful for what you did for our country during your many years of distinguished service in World War II, Korea, and Vietnam. We're also in your debt for the role you played in Texas and America in general in the Texan's War on Drugs.

Yes, family, General Risner is quite a man, and he certainly has done and is doing a lot for our country. At a time when we have a shortage of heroes, I wanted to remind you and our readers that as long as America produces some

Robinson Risners along the way, we will remain free and strong.

Love,

DAD

Question: *What is love?*

Answer: *Love is giving people hope.*

A GOOD RESOLUTION

Dear Family (and everybody else),

I had quite an experience on my way to Ohio this week. The little town where I spoke does not have a big airport and is served only by commuter lines. I flew into Pittsburgh, Pennsylvania, from Dallas and had a two-hour layover. I started down to the gate a full hour early. On the way I passed a shoeshine stand and decided to get a shine.

There were two young men shining shoes. One was a happy-go-lucky, outgoing, personable, extroverted sort of guy. The other was quiet and reserved, never smiling or saying anything. I secretly hoped that things would work out for me to get the happy guy. As it worked out, I drew the other one. But you know me and my inclination to cheer people up, especially if they are in a position of service.

As I stepped up into the chair, I cheerfully said to the young man, "Well, how ya doin'?" He looked at me without comment or even any indication that I'd spoken. No smile, no greeting, no nothing. I'll have to confess that I thought to myself that here was a guy who just wasn't using his head. A large portion of his income must come from tips, and tips are primarily determined by the relationship he establishes with the person he serves. I was astonished that he did not at least acknowledge my presence.

Then he went to work on my shoes. As he put on the saddle soap to clean them, I couldn't help but notice that he was meticulous and thorough. So I thought to myself, "Well, maybe I'll get a good shine and, after all, that's what I want and need." As he finished cleaning the shoes and started to brush them, I grudgingly admitted that not only was he careful and thorough, but he obviously knew what he was doing and was actually very good.

It wasn't until he had finished brushing the shoes and started applying the shine cloth to them that I really realized just how skillful he was. As he silently ran that cloth back and forth to put a high shine on my shoes, I listened carefully and began hearing some almost inaudible grunts. Then for the first time I really looked at the young man. It was obvious that he was a seriously disadvantaged young man with a minimum I.Q.

If I have ever felt like I wanted to just disappear, it was at that precise moment. Here I was making superficial judgments, condemning the young man for not being outgoing, personable, and grateful, and pondering whether I should "honor" him by letting him shine my shoes. All this time he was doing something that very few of us do. He was using his ability to the fullest. He was taking pride in his work and shining my shoes in a highly professional manner.

I made a resolution that day that I would be less judgmental of others and the efforts they expend in life. The old Indian admonition that we not judge another until we've "walked in his moccasins for two days" is certainly applicable here.

Not only did the young man teach me a lesson, which periodically I have to relearn, but I believe he offers a lesson to anyone who is willing to learn. I have no idea what the young man's income might be but I have a strong suspicion it's pretty good. I know as far as I'm concerned he got the biggest tip I had ever given anyone for shining my shoes. He also received my fervent prayers after I'd asked God to forgive me for my haughty, judgmental attitude.

Love,

DAD

Remember:　*Man looks on the outward appearance but God looks on the heart.*

Love is:　*Looking with love and compassion at the good qualities present in everyone.*

Part III

REARING SUCCESSFUL, WELL-ADJUSTED CHILDREN

TALKING "UP" TO THE KIDS

Dear Suzie, Julie, Chad, Jim, and all other parents,

In recent months an incredible amount of information has been published indicating that when babies are born they comprehend a great deal of what goes on around them. That's one of the reasons it pleases me so much to see you playing and talking to Keeper and Sunshine as you do. Even though they are now four and seven years old, respectively, it's exciting to know that from the moment of birth you've talked to and played with them.

Evidence is irrefutable that when you first take those babies in your arms and start kissing, cooing, and talking to them, you're having an intellectual as well as an emotional impact on their lives.

I once thought your mother was overdoing it when she used grown-up language with two-year-olds. However, research, as reported in *Psychology Today,* as well as the book, *The Secret Life of Your Unborn Child* by Thomas Verny and John Kelly, firmly establishes the fact that brand-new babies comprehend a great deal, even though they can't communicate what they understand.

You girls might recall that when you were first learning to talk we taught you a number of phrases which you could not understand, but which you parroted at our insistence. One of my favorites was the response we taught you to the question, "What is frost?" Your response: "Frozen precipitation caused by atmospheric conditions." While technically this might not be 100 percent accurate, the phrase was important in your education. (Incidentally, I have to confess that part of my motivation was "showing you off.")

At an early age you learned how to say words far beyond your understanding. This gave you some valuable mental gymnastics to perform. The real message I want to communicate is for you to keep on talking to your children. Do as your mother does—talk to them as "big people," while hugging, kissing, and loving them as "little people." You should talk slowly and more distinctly, and remember to repeat and rephrase your words for emphasis. This will help to combat some of the incredibly childish and immature language they will see on television and hear from some of the people we all must associate with in our lifetime.

Love,

DAD

> Fact: *The* input *into your child's life today will have considerable impact on your child's* output *tomorrow.*

VOCABULARY
IS IMPORTANT

Dear Family and everybody else,

As you undoubtedly recall, some time ago we saw a tremendous amount of publicity coming out of Girard, Pennsylvania. It had to do with the fact that some parents violently objected to the fact that their children were being required to read the book, *Working,* by Studs Terkel. The book contains some highly offensive language to which these parents strongly objected. They were not out to burn or ban the book; they simply were insisting that their children be given alternative reading. They felt, and rightly so, that since their children were not permitted to indulge in that kind of barnyard language at home, they should not be required by the school to read it.

There was considerable publicity about the matter, and Studs Terkel himself vigorously defended his book. While on a speaking engagement in Washington, I picked up a copy of the *Washington Post* and read an editorial comment concerning the incident. This particular writer was taking the position that it was absolutely absurd for these parents to object to that kind of language. He pointed out, with considerable accuracy, that in the "real world" that kind of language is very common and in everyday use. His position was that by reading this kind of language the kids would be better prepared to "live in the real world," where not only filthy language, but violent acts of rape, murder, and assault are everyday occurrences. Again, he was right. Those occurrences are common.

My position, however, is somewhat different. If you want to prepare your kids to go out and live in a world of drugs, filthy language, and violence, then perhaps you should give them that kind of exposure. I just happen to believe that education should serve a much higher purpose. I believe that we should educate our children on a high moral plane with good, clean, pure, powerful, and positive language. This approach will not prepare our students to live in that filth-filled, violent society. Education's purpose should be, must be, to prepare our young people to change society for the better. The goal should be to improve and elevate society so we can rebuild America to its former position of international trust and respect.

If I were commissioned to destroy a nation, I would start by changing its vocabulary. Words build you up *or* tear you down. Words paint pictures of end results and can bring smiles of joy and peace or frowns of horror or distress. As management expert Joe Batten challenges audiences with certain words, so shall I challenge you with those same words: *Vomit... Incest... Decapitation... Disembowel.* Well, what do you think?

Now let's look at some other words that have a different impact: *Love... Giving... Hope... Green meadows.* Words do make a difference, don't they? (Words of filth and violence out of the barnyard and gutter will ultimately bring an individual's or a nation's thinking down to the gutter or barnyard level. Neither the individual nor the nation can long remain higher than its thinking, which can be expressed only by the words we use.)

Words either build up or tear down, so these are some of the reasons you never heard your mother or me use foul or abusive language. This also explains why words like "dumb" or "stupid" were never part of our vocabulary, and it's why — even before I knew Jesus Christ on a personal basis — I would never take His name in vain.

On this same wavelength, I agree with psychologist Bruno Bettelheim of the University of Chicago who says we should teach our children fairy tales. In fairy tales, Dr. Bettelheim says, the lines are clearly drawn between the good guy and the bad guy, and the good guy always wins. He points out that even the kids know that this is not what always happens, but deep down they know that it is right and is what ought to happen so they are inspired to go to work and make it happen.

That's my position exactly. I believe that in raising each of you our prime function should have been — and has been — to raise you in a highly moral manner so that you can go out into the world and help take it forward with a positive contribution. Those individuals who live in that negative, violent, immoral society will see there is a better way. The testimony of your lives will help them to a better way of life and living. Ultimately, that approach will build a better America.

I would be willing to debate anyone on the merits of this approach.

Love,

DAD

DOING WHAT'S BEST
FOR THE KIDS

Dear Ziglar Children and everybody else,

Sometimes we know things and we know they're right, but we don't really know why and how we know they are right. You will remember that as you grew up you were never permitted to talk back to or "put down" either your mother or your dad. Both of us had been raised by loving, Bible-oriented, Christian mothers who administered discipline and demanded courtesy and respect.

I just finished reading a revealing article in *Psychology Today* by Dr. Bruno Bettelheim. He pointed out that when a child is permitted to put the parent down it destroys the child. The child's sense of confidence and security grows when he can trust his parents and depend on them to be strong and reliant. By putting the parent down, the child elevates himself to a position above the parent. His security then evaporates because a child can't look up to someone he's just put down (he might fear the parent, but that's entirely different).

As a child goes through life, and especially as he reaches puberty, he will encounter many situations when direction from a mom and/or dad he loves and respects will mean the difference between winning in life or losing much of life. Proper direction can and often does make the difference in a moral or immoral lifestyle, in getting an education, or in settling for immediate, but often very temporary, benefits.

Those are some of the reasons your mother and I have tried to be good, strong role models for you. Truthfully, we want to be your heroes. That's why we have never tried to be your buddies. We believe your buddies should be from your own age group. We never treated you as equals because a five- or ten-year-old child is not equal to his thirty- or forty-year-old parent, either in judgment or experience. In God's sight our souls are equal. But He is clear in His instructions that children are to obey their parents and that parents are to love their children so much that they will do what is best for each child.

Your mom and I always believed you needed role models, parents you could look up to in love and respect. Don't misunderstand. By no stretch of the imagination do we believe we're always right and you're always wrong. Far from it! We know that you have some answers we do not have, but we still insist that from birth the child should display respect for the parent. This is not a question of intellect, but of experience.

We feel strongly about our role as parents because God tells us in His Book that we are responsible for preparing you for the trials and opportunities of life. The best way to do that is to demand respect and obedience from you as toddlers and then earn love and respect from you as you enter adolescence.

I hope you know that we love, admire, and respect each one of you for who and what you are. Without exception, we seek advice from all four of you on various matters, just as you do from us. In the final analysis, however, we wanted to give you the security of knowing that you had parents whom you could love and depend on to act in your best interests.

We felt that the best training for your future leadership and parental roles was to observe leadership on a day-to-day basis from the moment of birth. By observation you can learn what is good, what is bad, and what the basic difference is. To do this, however, you need a role model you can love and respect — not a "buddy" you can challenge.

To a lesser degree in our educational system and in our law enforcement structure, when citizens or students are permitted to be insolent, challenging, disrespectful, vulgar, and antagonistic towards authority positions, it is the individual who is seriously damaged. If we have no respect for law, who is Joe Citizen going to look to for trust and protection? How can you look to an officer you've just cursed and abused and put down to protect you from the criminal element in society?

As parents we often have fallen short, but we have tried to set good examples because, as your grandmother said, "Set a good example and you won't have to set many rules." Now that all of you are adults and two of you have children of your

own, I hope you will set the kind of example your children
will be proud to follow.

Love,

DAD

Thought: *Remember that you can't put anyone else
"down" without joining them at a lower level.
Nor can you build anyone "up" without
joining them at a higher level.*

Mama Ziglar's
Sermonette: *Your children more attention pay
To what you do than what you say.*

REMOVING GUILT
WITH DISCIPLINE

Dear Tom (and all other boys and girls),

Well, this has been "one of those days," Son. I don't know
what happened, but as the day wore on it got worse and
worse. You were in quite a challenging mood, and on several
occasions you did everything but openly defy me. As we have
frequently heard people say, you were "asking for it." I couldn't
believe my son, who was nearly twelve, was saying and doing
those things.

Finally at about 3:15 P.M. you took the step that carried
you over the line. At that point I reached for my belt, and
several well-aimed, firm, but not abusive, licks on your well-
padded posterior achieved remarkable results. After the shed-
ding of a few tears, followed by hugging and my assuring

you that I loved you, you were about the happiest boy I have ever seen.

Psychologists tell us, Son, that when a child has done something he knows is wrong the action *demands* discipline. The rebellion or wrongdoing leaves a definite feeling of guilt in the child, and if he is permitted to "get away with it," his feelings of guilt are not relieved. The result is an uneasy, unhappy child carrying a burden that grows progressively heavier.

You had been asking—even pleading with—me to remove that guilt. When I neglected to give you the discipline you asked for, those guilt feelings built and built until you reached the breaking point. Then, when I did what needed to be done and you had "paid the price" for having been rebellious and disobedient, the deck was cleared. At that point nothing stood between either you and your dad or you and a clear conscience. You were free to go your own way.

That was over seven years ago, Son, and that's the last time I had to get my belt. Obviously, I don't ever expect to do it again, but the requirements for conforming with the rules and regulations of the household and continuing to honor and respect your mom and dad will always stay the same.

Love,

DAD

Thought: *"Spare the rod and spoil the child" is as valid today as it ever was. A 1980 Gallup Poll revealed that over 90 percent of our high school seniors wish parents and teachers loved them enough to discipline them more and expect more from them.*

P.S. *The belt was applied firmly but without anger. Certainly there were no marks left, and I doubt that even a pinkish glow existed for more than fifteen minutes. This action, Son, was taken for you and was not done to you. It was discipline, not punishment.*

AS YE SOW, SO ALSO SHALL YE REAP

Dear Tom (and everybody else),

Decisions and actions you take today will influence your life for years to come. They may influence your children and even your grandchildren. As you know, I have great love and respect for my mother. She always told us that you couldn't be almost honest; you either were, or you were not.

Recently I received a lengthy letter from your Aunt Jewel and Uncle Huie, who subscribe to that idea 100 percent. As you might recall, Uncle Huie's son, Jack, recently lost his job after nearly nineteen years with a large motor line because the company went out of business. Jack has a serious heart condition so, at age forty-one it was really tough for him to get another job. At that age, insurance considerations and the potential liability of a heart problem were more than most companies wanted to tackle. So for several months Jack futilely sought a job. Then one day he received a telephone call from a man who had heard he was looking for work. He invited Jack to come in for an interview. The man's name sounded familiar, but Jack couldn't place him until he walked into his office.

Twenty-three years earlier they had gone to night school together and had worked in the same grocery store. Jack's friend was now a successful businessman and remembered something about Jack that prompted the phone call. He remembered that several young men had worked in the grocery store with him, but Jack was the only other one who did not steal from the employer. When he heard that Jack was seeking work he immediately called him because, as he expressed it, "We always need a man who is completely honest."

That's the message in this letter. When you play the game of life like it ought to be played—which is straight—sooner or later you're going to reap the benefits. There are a lot of ways your grandmother would express that sentiment. She would start by quoting God's Word: "As ye sow, so also shall ye reap." Then she might well throw in the "Bread cast upon the waters . . . " routine. I guess it all boils down to the fact that you decide what kind of crop you want later in life and plant the proper seeds today.

Love,

DAD

Thought: *The time is always right to do the right thing.*

CHILDREN SEE, CHILDREN DO

Dear Ziglar Children (and All Ambitious People),

Today I heard a commercial discussing vocabulary and the declining reading skills of society caused in part by television and electronic games. As I listened, I thought of each one of you and noted with considerable satisfaction that without exception all of you enjoy reading good books and good magazines to acquire worthwhile information and inspiration. I've a strong feeling that one of the reasons you enjoy reading is because all of your lives you have seen your mother and dad regularly reading good literature.

We do pick up habits from our parents. It's well-documented that parents who smoke, drink, and use drugs are far more likely to have children who also smoke, drink, and use drugs. According to *Parade* magazine, if a youngster's parents are both obese, the chances are 85 percent that the youngster himself will become obese. It is not because obesity is inherited, but because in watching his parents overeat, he will follow suit. Sometimes the parents mistakenly urge their children to continue to eat long after they have satisfied their needs, but often the kids learn from watching the parents indulge themselves. Example *is* the best—or at least the most effective— teacher, so when kids see their parents constantly overeat, smoke, drink, or use drugs, the inclination to follow suit is strong. Fortunately, good habits such as reading can also be picked up by watching parents over a period of time.

To enhance your reading skill and to increase your education, I also encourage you to learn a new word every day. I recommend *Reader's Digest,* because each month it has a section featuring thirty new words. I'm absolutely convinced that anyone who learns those thirty new words a month—or one word per day—will be fairly well-educated within five years, regardless of his educational background. I'm *positive* that statement applies to any reader who has read this far in this book. We know that every word has a lot of buddies. You learn how to use one new word today, and later you will be able to identify it with other words. Thus, your vocabulary grows.

The International Paper Company proved beyond any doubt that a person's vocabulary has a direct bearing on his income. The reason is simple: You express your thoughts with words, and if you do not have the words at your command, it is difficult to express your thoughts. Communication is a critical factor to advancement in our modern society. So, Kids, keep reading, keep studying those words, and "I'll *See You at the Top!*"

Love,

DAD

Thought: *If you think education is expensive, have you checked on the price of ignorance?*

BARBERS AND DENTISTS: FRIENDS OR FOES?

Dear Ziglar Children—and all others who grow up—

Growing up can be a painful experience because of the tremendous number of unknown factors. Your mother and I have enjoyed watching each of you grow up. You might not remember, but your mother and I did a couple of things with you that made sense and spared you some fears and tears, as well as some embarrassment for all of us.

In your case, Tom, when you were less than two years old I started taking you to the barber shop and letting you sit in my lap for a moment or two while the barber cut my hair. You quickly saw that having the sheet over me was not a frightening or painful experience. After two or three trips, I encouraged the barber to take a small snip of your hair and then show you what he had done. A few trips were all that was required, Son, and when you started getting haircuts there never were those painful and embarrassing, screaming, tear-shedding episodes I have often witnessed in barber shops.

Trips to the beauty shop for the girls were quite different because by the time you girls were old enough to go, you were ready, willing, able, and anxious to go—with one exception. The exception was Suzan, and she was quite an exception! She fought her first trip to the beauty shop like she was fighting for her life. She had beautiful long, blonde hair, but it was lots of trouble. Your mother felt strongly that it would look better if it were cut shorter. Finally, when Suzan was thirteen, mother dragged her screaming, crying, and clawing to the beauty shop (that is literally the truth). During the operation (haircut), big old crocodile tears rolled down our "little" girl's cheeks. Fortunately, she did survive.

Trips to the dentist were almost the same story. Your mother took all four of you (one at a time, of course). Basically, she followed the same procedure with the dentist that I used with the barber.

Each of you would sit in her lap a moment or two while the dentist took care of the preliminaries with her. Then the dentist would pat your head and speak pleasantly to you. On the next trip he would open your mouth and put his mirror and one of his little instruments inside and wiggle it around as he smiled and laughed with you. When your mother was ready to leave, she made certain she was laughing and very pleasant with him. The entire experience came across to each of you as fun rather than terrifying.

When each of you made your first trip to the dentist for treatment, it was a good one. As a matter of fact, all the dentist did was examine your teeth to see how you were doing. The second trip was a cleaning trip, but on the third one he got down to serious business and filled a couple of teeth. At this point another exception popped up.

When the dentist was seriously working on Cindy, she still

had her "baby" teeth, which usually do not require an anesthetic. The result was disastrous because he hit a nerve and our Cindy came out of the chair. It was a painful and traumatic experience, and for two or three years it was like pulling teeth to get her back to the dentist—any dentist. As a matter of fact, the only way we could handle the situation was to give her a tranquilizer before your mother could get her into the car for the trip to the dentist.

Fortunately, you other three children had good experiences with the dentists, and we are grateful for that. Like I say, it's exciting to watch your children grow.

Love,

DAD

Thought: *Preparing your children properly to face social and life situations without fear or embarrassment will speed and simplify their entrance into the real world.*

Fact: *Regardless of how well you plan and prepare your children in the "laboratory" at home, since every child is different they won't always perform according to the book when they face life beyond the nest. That's why time, love and common sense are important ingredients in the success formula for raising well-adjusted children.*

TAKING CARE OF THE LITTLE ONES

Dear Suzie (and all other loving parents and grandparents),

On the way to the airport today the traffic was awfully heavy and moved in stops and jerks. As I was driving along I noticed a lady holding her baby—who appeared to be about eight or ten months old—in her arms as she drove. I thought back to my own early parenthood when I held you and your little sisters and brother on my lap as we drove around town, (one at a time, of course) looking the proud father, showing off his offspring.

Then I remembered that about three months ago I wanted to take Katherine Jean Alexandra Witmeyer (better known as "Keeper") with me to the grocery store. You looked at me and said, "Okay, Dad, but we'll have to move the car seat to your car for her." I explained that the grocery store was only two blocks away and you replied that two blocks was plenty of room to have an accident.

Of course, you were right. As I looked at that lady with her baby it came through loud and clear that if she should have a sudden impact, her baby could be crushed between her body and the steering wheel. At that moment, Doll, I was awfully proud and grateful that you're taking such good care of my granddaughter.

Love,

DAD

Thought: *It's better to be safe today than sorry for a lifetime.*

Procedure: *Do what is best for your children—even if it*

> *means sacrificing a little pleasure for you or making life a little more complicated.*

EVERYONE WORKS FOR HIMSELF

Dear Family (and everybody else),

We've often talked about whether it's better to be in your own business or "work for someone else." Actually, one of the saddest and most misguided notions we've ever embraced in our society is the erroneous idea that most people work for someone else. This just isn't true. Oh, I'll agree that most people receive a paycheck from an employer for services they render or work they've done, but I'm going to insist that no one ever works for anyone else. The boss or employer might sign the check, but *you* ultimately will fill in the amount. We all work for ourselves, and each of us wants to be paid for our efforts so we can use at least part of the money for our personal benefit.

Most of us like to feel we're making a contribution, and I strongly believe that you can get everything in life you want if you will just help enough other people get what they want. Here's my point. The harder and more effectively you work, the greater the rewards are going to be. Even though someone else might sign your paycheck, your performance and your attitude will determine the amount they put on that check.

When you show up for work on time, do what you are supposed to do, and leave the job on time with your check in hand, everybody is even. You were hired out and paid off.

Nobody owes anybody anything. That's the reason it's critical you understand that when you get to work early and demonstrate an extra amount of enthusiasm in your job and do far more than you're being paid to do, you're really working for yourself. Eventually the boss will see what you're doing and reward you appropriately.

He won't reward you because he is benevolent. He will reward you with a raise because he understands that you are truly a rare individual. He also understands that if he doesn't pay you for the extra effort, somebody down the street will see what you're doing and offer to pay you what you deserve. That's what's so great about America and the free enterprise system. Regardless of your race, creed, or color, you can plan your future. You can write your own ticket to the top.

I'm confident all of you understand what I'm talking about when I say that you really do work for yourself. Take it seriously, children, and you'll find that life's fun, exciting, *and* rewarding.

Love,

DAD

Message: *The boss might not always be looking, so you can temporarily fool him. However, you are always looking and you can never fool you. Do your best, and I'll guarantee it will be good enough.*

Thought: *When you do more than you are paid to do, you will eventually be paid more for what you do.*

TELEVISION,
THE GREAT TEACHER

Dear Family (and everybody else),

From time to time we've talked about the impact television has had and is having on our moral values. We've discussed the direction we, as individuals, and our country are taking as a result. When you turn the set on, the teaching or selling begins immediately. As an example, let's look at what *U.S. News and World Report* says about advertising.

The average twenty-year-old American has seen one million television commercials. That translates into fifty thousand per year, or one thousand per week. Most of these commercials involve solutions to problems in thirty to sixty seconds. They range from sleepless nights, which are easily cured by one product; dateless weekends solved by another product; to nervousness and irritability, which are remedied by yet another product. The list is endless.

The basic problem this creates is that when kids get to be about nine or ten years old, the teachers start to ask questions that do not have thirty-to-sixty-second solutions. At this point many kids realize that life is not really that easy, and they begin to withdraw.

Some of them camp in front of the television set even more. Others sleep more, while many find comfort in gorging themselves on junk food. By far the most serious problem, however, is the escape route many of the youngsters take into drugs, alcohol, and sexual immorality. The result is that today we have over 5 million youngsters seventeen years old and under who smoke pot on a daily basis and 5.3 million of our young people seventeen and under who have serious drinking problems. Additionally, venereal disease and teenage pregnancy are epidemic.

At this point I know it looks like I'm blaming television for all our problems and, to a degree, I suppose I am. However, I am completely aware of the fact that all television sets have an "off" button that needs to be used more often.

Even more desirable is the "out" position which daughter Suzan and her husband, Chad, have taken. In the last three years I have talked with approximately two hundred families who have also taken their television sets out of their homes. Without exception, they tell me that after the first few days, during which the family adjusts to the shock, removing the television set was the smartest thing they had ever done.

They elaborate on how neat it is to be able to finish a meal, a visit, or a shopping trip and not have to hurry so they won't miss some program. They say it's great to be able to talk without having to wait for a commercial or rush home from work in time to watch the six o'clock news; that it is really neat to have someone drop in and you don't have to finish the program before you can visit. Without exception these families tell me that they are much, much closer, the children's grades are definitely better, and discipline is much easier.

Don't misunderstand. Television is not all bad, but at least we should be selective in our viewing habits. This little example points out the impact television has on our thinking.

My son-in-law, Chad Witmeyer, recently had surgery, and while recuperating at home he asked one of his friends to bring him a television set so he could watch the football games. Naturally, Keeper was in on part of the watching and, as you undoubtedly know, the beer people with their athletic heroes as spokesmen are prime sponsors of those National Football League games. One morning after just a few days of television viewing, noticing her daddy's discomfort, Keeper looked at him and asked, "What's the matter, Daddy? Don't you feel good?" Before he could answer she continued, "Do you want me to bring you a Miller Lite?" I leave all the implications to your own imagination, but I know you'll agree that television does have an impact.

I do not believe now—nor have I ever believed—that we treat our young people fairly when we delude them into believing that life is a bowl of cherries, that it's easy and full of sixty-second solutions.

One of the most moving examples of the advantages of no television came to me on May 20, 1981. My associate, Jim Savage, and I went to Cleveland, Wisconsin, for a speaking engagement and met an unusual young administrator named Steve Smith who shared the following story.

Steve and his wife, Ginny, had decided to be very selective in watching their television set and spend more time with their son. Immediately after they made this move, Steve started taking his son for walks in the community. After two or three days another little guy joined them. A couple of days later yet another came along, until finally Steve looked like the Pied Piper of Manitowoc, Wisconsin.

After this had been going on for a few weeks, Steve and Ginny were seated inside their home one afternoon with the windows open and their seven-year-old was just outside the window playing with one of his buddies. In a few moments the little buddy casually and off-the-cuff asked Steve's son why his daddy had so much time to go for walks and play with him. Steve's son rather matter-of-factly said, "We don't watch much television anymore." After a few seconds the little buddy rather wistfully commented, "I wish we didn't watch so much television so my daddy could play with me more."

It is tragic that that little guy had a daddy, but that daddy had a television set that he remembered—and a son whom he forgot.

Love,

DAD

Question: *Do you control your television set and its use,
or does the television set control you?*

HOW DO WE KEEP OUR
KIDS OFF DRUGS?

Dear Suzan, Cindy, and Julie,

Over the years we have talked a lot about drugs, and on
many occasions you have asked questions about what you can
do to make certain your children never get involved with
them. That's a big question, so let's take a look at the drug
scene and what it involves.

As you know, you can't pick up a newspaper today without
reading about drugs because the problem is enormous. Over
the years I've had a chance to meet and know addicts, ex-
addicts, and parents of addicts. Never do I talk with one who
has been brought out of the horror of drugs that I don't hear
words of gratitude and in virtually every case expressions of
their faith, which was the saving and sustaining force. This is
true not only of the kids who were hooked but of the parents
as well.

First Lady Nancy Reagan is taking the drug war directly to
the people and is giving much hope and encouragement to
parents and victims all over America. Our government is
waging a relentless war on smugglers and pushers. I'm
delighted and enthusiastic at such interest, not only of our
government, but of concerned citizen groups all over America.

Unfortunately, there is no way we're going to completely
stop the flow of drugs. They've become entrenched in our
society, and the dollars simply are too big for us to stop the

supply. However, we can substantially *reduce* the supply and dramatically lower the demand.

I'm totally convinced, based on everything I've seen in over twelve years of dealing with the problem, that if we will teach youngsters from birth about the horrors of drugs, we can and will get results. Yes, fear can motivate and emphatically does work at the younger level.

In our school system from kindergarten through high school we must make the danger clear about the damage that tobacco, pot, alcohol, and the other mind-altering drugs can do to a person physically, mentally, financially, and spiritually. In our I Can course now being taught in over 3,500 schools from kindergarten through college, more than 28 percent of the young people on drugs were able to stop taking them by the time they completed the course. More importantly, a significantly higher percentage of those young people who had never tried drugs made the decision while in the course never to get involved in drugs. To my way of thinking, the way to solve the problem is to get to the kids with the truth before their "friends" reach them with lies.

Now, obviously, we don't just deal with the negative of why no one should get involved in drugs. More importantly, we deal in the positive aspects and sell our young people on the fact that a drug-free life offers more long-range pleasure and happiness while preparing them for the opportunity to take advantage of the American Dream.

One great truth is that "Man was designed for accomplishment, engineered for success, and endowed with the seeds of greatness." Once we have elevated the self-images of our youngsters and taught them how to set and reach worthwhile goals and how to develop a winning attitude, they will have no need to get involved in drugs. They will like themselves and will not "need" to chemically change to "be like everybody else" to gain acceptance. Self-acceptance largely negates the need for acceptance by others.

It's not enough just to say that I've never seen a successful addict, nor a happy one. We need to accentuate the positive and let all our young people know that by keeping our minds and bodies clean and healthy we can have more fun and get infinitely more out of life.

Here are some other particulars that will be helpful. According to Dr. Forest Tennant (who runs the largest drug clinic in America with the largest group of research assistants, and has the most complete statistical data on drugs in America), there are four things parents can do to help keep their kids from getting involved with drugs: Number one, spank them regularly, moderately, and without anger when they blatantly rebel and disobey. Number two, *take* them to church fifty or more times by the time they are fifteen years old. Number three, set the right example for the kids, meaning that parents must not get involved in the smoking, drinking, drug scene themselves. Number four, absolutely forbid the child to smoke until at least age eighteen. You can enforce this at home.

According to Dr. Tennant, if we can solve the smoking problem we will largely have solved the drug problem. His reasoning is simple: over 95 percent of the kids who smoke pot started with cigarettes, and over 95 percent of the people who go on to cocaine and heroin smoked pot along the way.

Dr. Tennant *did not* say that everyone who smokes cigarettes moves on to pot and heroin. He *did* say that if a person smokes pot the odds are about nineteen to one that he started with cigarettes. The reason is simple: You must know how to inhale in order to smoke pot, and smoking cigarettes teaches one how. As Dr. Tennant declares, "Educate our young people on the damage and dangers of tobacco, and we will have largely solved the drug problem."

Incidentally, Dr. Tennant also says it is pure idiocy for anyone to think a youngster can be "taught" to drink. He points out that the three countries with the highest rates of wine consumption in the world are France, Italy, and Chile; the highest rates of cirrhosis of the liver are in France, Italy, and Chile. Would you believe that by "coincidence" the three highest rates of alcoholism in the world are France, Italy, and Chile? You should, because it's a fact!

Along these same lines, it is a tragic fact that teenage alcoholism has increased over 300 percent since the "hard sell" approach to selling beer and wine on television by athletic heroes started some twenty years ago. This makes it especially difficult to understand why *millions* of parents don't write the Federal Communications Commission (1919 M Street Northwest, Washington, D.C. 20554), and demand that beer and wine commercials be taken off television as the cigarette commercials were.

I know this is a lengthy letter, but the subject matter demands specific instructions.

Love,

DAD

P.S. *Regardless of where cigarette smoking takes you as far as other drugs are concerned, we know that it will take over 350,000 Americans out of this life prematurely this year. We also know that every time you light up you just chose to die fourteen minutes earlier.*

A VALUABLE ASSET:
YOUR TEMPER

Dear Suzan, Cindy, Julie, and all other "temper losers,"

There was one thing that happened in each of your lives. Each one of you lost one of your most valuable possessions — your temper. *Our temper is extremely valuable.* You were very young and had not learned to control it yourselves. Therefore, it was my responsibility as your father to help you control that temper until you matured enough to handle it on your own.

The cause of your temper tantrums has long since been forgotten, but in these incidents each one of you threw yourself on the floor, kicked your feet, and slapped the floor with your hands. In your case, Cindy, you also added a little head-bumping to the process. My procedure in each case was the same. I picked you up, made quite an impression on you with a little loving bottom-warming (no bruises, just a mild, pink glow), and sent you on your way. In each of your cases, one serious temper tantrum was all you had.

In your case, Cindy, you *almost* had the second one, which I'll never forget. Not long after the first incident something else happened, and again you threw yourself on the floor. You got so far as to draw back to kick and bang your head. Then suddenly you apparently remembered what happened the first time you did this, because you cut your eyes at me with a look that clearly said, "Oh, my goodness! What have I done?" You immediately proceeded to hop up and scoot out of the room. Your mother and I thought it was hilarious, but I was especially relieved that I wasn't going to have to use any more applied psychology. You were about six years old, and as I remember that was one of the last times you even came close to needing a spanking. You girls were and are fast learners!

That was part of the passing parade of life, and I just wanted you to know that I'm glad each of you found your tempers and thought so much of them that you decided to keep them.

Love,

DAD

Message: *Many times, to steal a line from Christian psychologist Henry Brandt, our kids need help. I believe that if our kids "lose" their tempers we need to immediately get busy and help them "find" this valuable possession.*

Thought: *By learning to keep your temper as a child, you greatly reduce the danger of losing it later in life when the loss could also cause you to lose a friend, a job, a mate, or even your life.*

SOME THINGS TO GET EXCITED ABOUT

Dear Family (and everybody else),

Recently I was in Edmonton, Alberta, and heard my friend, Jim Janz, make a speech. He said a lot of good things with which I agree, but one thing struck me as particularly significant.

Jim pointed out that in a football game, if it's third down and three yards to go for a first down in a close game, the local partisans will stand up and cheer their team onward. When the running back hits the line with full force and the issue is in doubt, the officials bring the measuring chain to the center of the field to determine whether he just made it or just missed it. If he made the three yards, the stands erupt in a tremendous burst of energy, excitement, and enthusiasm. They rant, rave, whoop, and holler as if an earth-shattering event had just taken place. Yep, they really get excited about a three-yard gain in a football game.

Now, family, I find no fault with that excitement. But, as Jim pointed out, if we can get that excited about a football game, why can't we get excited about something *really* important? As you know, I'm excited about a lot of things. I'm excited because I have the privilege of serving my God. I'm excited because I live in America, the greatest land on the face of this earth. I'm excited that I am free and have an opportunity to come and go as I please and pursue my own interests. I'm excited about my family.

My whole point is simply that it seems so absurd that today there are some who think it a little strange that I exhibit enthusiasm for the really important things in life, and yet they exhibit enthusiasm when the runner makes a first down on third and three. They show enthusiasm over many things that will have no bearing on anything of significance. They even arrange their schedule so they can be in front of the television set to watch a program with negative or minimal benefits. Yet many of these same people show little or no real excitement for their families, their opportunities, their country, or their God. What a tragedy!

Yes, our sense of values in our society is really distorted, isn't it? Jim Janz was right, and I thank him for reminding me that we have much to be excited about. The more excitement we display for things that are important, the more people will see the importance of these things and join us in our excitement.

Love,

DAD

Message: *Get excited about* important *things: your child's improvement in manners, appearance, or grades; your mate's birthday or commitment to family or community service; the fish your son caught, or your daughter's piano recital. In short, get excited about the daily incidents that are exciting and that* will *make a difference in a life.*

DO YOU "LOSE" OR GET BEAT?

Dear Tom (and everybody else),

It's amazing what happens when a boy grows up. It's also exciting when that boy shares many interests with his dad. I love to play golf with you, Son, because not only are you an excellent competitor, but you are now beating your dad like a drum. Don't misunderstand. I don't like to be beaten, but there is a difference in "losing" and being beaten. You "lose" when you do less than your best and come out on the short end of the score. You "lose" when you blame the greens, weather, fairways, bad bounces, lousy rules, slow golfers, new putters, an old driver, and everything else under the sun for your miserable score.

The scorecard will show that you beat me the last twenty-plus times we've played, but the bigger scorecard of life will show that I "won" every time we teed up. I "won," Son, because we spent several very pleasant and relaxing hours together. I "won" because we always talk about fun and pleasant things, as well as some of the more serious aspects of life. I "won" because the fresh air and relaxing nature of the game recharges my physical, mental, and spiritual batteries. I "won" because you've never seen me lose my temper and utter a profane word. You've never seen me throw a club or take any anger out on "innocent" golf balls or golf clubs after I missed a "gimme" putt or easy chip shot.

Don't misunderstand that last statement, either, because my competitive nature certainly doesn't jump with joy when I blow an easy shot and add to my score. Two important things are involved. First, I'm convinced it is not in my best interests to let a "game" get the best of me. Second, I believe I would let you down if I taught you, by example, that there is nothing wrong with losing your temper and acting like a spoiled seven-year-old when things don't go your way.

Another reason I "won," Son, is because you are a good student of the game and give me some helpful suggestions from time to time. As a matter of fact, the two most helpful hints I've had to improve my game came from you. I'm pleased that you are a good student, and I'm delighted that you can spot some flaws and offer constructive suggestions. There are many people who can tell you that "you missed the shot," or that you are wrong. Many people criticize much about life, but often they have neither the heart nor the head to offer help. I'm delighted you have the head so that you *can* help and the heart so that you *will* help.

DAD

Lesson: *An idea or skill doesn't care who owns it. Stay open for suggestions and ideas from other*

people, even members of your own family
*(*especially *members of your own family).*

THE WAY TO SOLVE
TEENAGE
UNEMPLOYMENT

Dear Tom (and all other employment-seeking teenagers),

All of your life you've heard some fairly standard, conservative, straight-laced discussion of values as they relate to
honesty, character, integrity, faith, love, dependability, loyalty,
and responsibility. Now, my son, you're sixteen years old and
eligible for the job market. I'd like to share with you a little
sales technique and give you additional information as to
why the right way is the best way and why a firm foundation
is the best preparation for getting a job and succeeding in
life.

When the average sixteen-year-old, who has never worked,
applies for a job, the employer will ask the question, "What
is your experience?" The answer has got to be that this is the
first job, and so the youngster has no experience. The high
teenage unemployment figures give eloquent testimony to
the probability that the unemployed, inexperienced teenager will stay unemployed and inexperienced.

Fortunately, Son, you've got a better answer to that "what
is your experience" question, and so does every other youngster who has had the experience of being taught good, moral
values from the beginning. To that experience I'm going to
add a little sales talk.

When the employer asks you about your experience, you

look at him and say, "Well, Sir, I've had sixteen years' experience in telling the truth and understanding the values that go with it. I've had sixteen years' experience of knowing that if I'm going to get and keep a job I must be at work on time and do what I'm supposed to do, while getting along well with the other employees in the firm. I've had sixteen years' experience of knowing that if I'm going to get ahead in the job, I've got to have a good attitude that will include looking for things to do rather than things to avoid. I know that if I expect to keep my job and get a raise that I must understand some of the basic principles of business.

"For example, I know that when I show up for work on time, do what I'm paid to do, and leave on time with my check in my hand, that we're all even. I was hired out, did the work and you paid me so nobody owes anybody anything. If I want a raise, I know I've got to get here a little early and do more than I'm paid to do. I know I should stay a little late because the law of supply and demand clearly says that if I do more than I'm paid to do you will end up paying me more for what I do." (As an aside, Son, let me point out that any employee who takes this extra-mile approach in his job will have the satisfaction and peace of mind that comes from doing his very best.)

"I've had sixteen years' experience in knowing that the only way you're going to be able to keep me on the payroll is for you to make a profit, so I plan to work hard to help you make a profit so I can keep my job. Sir, I believe that's the kind of experience you need in your business."

Then you go for the "close," Son, with this statement and question: "To be completely honest, Sir, I want a job and need a job. I make only one promise: I'll work so hard that the day will come when you will say with pride that you were the man who gave me my first job." Then you should pause slightly, look him directly in the eye, smile, and say, "I can start immediately—or would the first of the week be better?"

I can't guarantee the job, Son, because that company might not have an opening, but if you give that presentation enough times I'm confident you'll get a job fairly soon.

Now, of course, Tom, I don't expect you to say all of that with the opening question, but that is the basic message you need to communicate. If you will convey that information, I don't believe there's an employer in the country who would not be impressed. If that employer doesn't have a current need for an additional employee, I believe that with this approach your name would go to the very top of the list for the next job opening. I also believe that the prospective employer would be willing to help a youngster with this approach and this attitude to get a job with some other company. Think about it, Son. You've got the foundation; now start memorizing your sales talk and I believe you can get a job.

Love,

DAD

P.S. *For the other young men and women who will read this, the same thing will work for you, too.*

Thought: *Evidence is solid that this approach works. If you will help spread this concept by insisting that it be taught in schools and churches you will be actively solving a major problem in our society. Question: Will you help?*

A *SUCCESSFUL* MAN

Dear Family,

Here's a successful man.

On Monday, September 13, 1982, Martin Lovvorn went home to be with the Lord. I did not know him well, but from a distance I admired him greatly. He was busy with his family, in his business, and in the church. As superintendent of the seniors at the First Baptist Church for twenty-five years he did a marvelous job. He was especially effective and eloquent when he awarded the scholarships to the high school graduates each year.

Last night one of my fellow deacons who knew Martin well described him as a loving family man, respected businessman, loyal husband, supportive father, and especially "a prince of God," as he served our Lord in a beautiful, loving and unselfish way.

As he was speaking of Martin Lovvorn I was thinking to myself, "What an absolutely marvelous thing to be able to say about a fellow deacon or a fellow human being." As you know, I spend a great deal of my time talking about the seven areas of life in which we should have goals: physical, mental, spiritual, family, social, career, and financial. Last night as my fellow deacon described Martin Lovvorn I could not help but think that here was a man who was a success. He was a success as a husband and father. He was a success in the business world and in his relationships with his fellow man. More importantly, he was a success with his Lord. What an example he set for all of us.

Love,

DAD

FINISH THE JOB...
AND DO IT RIGHT

Dear Tom,

I could tell you weren't overly happy when I asked you to do a better job on the yard. I acknowledged that time had run out and that you were obviously in a hurry. There are a couple of things involved that I think are important to your future. First, you clearly understood that you were to cut the yard on Monday—Labor Day. You planned to go dove hunting, which you did from 7 A.M. until 12:30. Then, at 1:30 you and I headed for the golf course, and because it was crowded we didn't get home until 7:30 P.M.

You did an excellent job for the time allotted, but you simply did not allot yourself enough time. Now you might reasonably argue that had I not played golf with you that maybe you would not have played and therefore your time factor would have been longer. I can't buy that idea, Son, in case you thought of it. The reason is simple. At age seventeen, responsibility should be a very big word in your vocabulary. If you do not accept responsibility, your usefulness and desirability as an employee will be seriously reduced. For several years it has been your responsibility to do the yard. As you grow older, the yard should look better and better as a result of your added experience and commitment.

There's something else that is equally important: Whatever your job might be, to quote your Grandmother Ziglar, "When a task is once begun, leave it not until it's done; and be a matter great or small, do it well or not at all." That advice applies to everything, Son, whether it's making the bed, waxing your car, cutting the grass, or studying your lessons.

If you get careless in completing a task, the same thing

happens to you that happens when you get careless on the golf course. As you know, when you relax and lose your concentration, you frequently miss a shot, and that missed shot often costs you two or even three more shots. That's not the way to play championship golf, and to relax and get careless in the fulfillment of a responsibility is not the way to give championship performances in life.

You will recall that in an earlier letter I pointed out that in life you work for yourself. Even if someone else signs the check, you ultimately fill in the amount of the check by virtue of your performance. The surest way to get ahead in life and pay yourself the maximum is to do the best you know how to do, regardless of what you're doing. Form these habits now, Son, and when you get into the work world doing your best will be second nature for you. Your best is going to be good enough to please most employers. Less than your best is another matter.

I'm the first employer to pay you for your work, and I want to be able to give you a good recommendation — not because you're my son, but because you're a good worker.

Love,

DAD

Thought: *Doing your best, regardless of the job, isn't just right — it's smart.*

QUESTION: CAN
—AND SHOULD—
EMPLOYERS
"DISCRIMINATE"
AGAINST SMOKERS?

Dear Tom,

You asked me why I feel so strongly about smoking. I'm glad you asked, and I'm even happier that you don't smoke. Here's why.

This year some 350,000-plus Americans will die prematurely because of smoking. The financial cost to society runs to an incredible 59 billion dollars. That's 21 billion dollars for buying the tobacco; 25 billion dollars because of lost productivity from the tobacco; and 13 billion dollars to treat tobacco-induced illnesses. Obviously, if we had 59 billion dollars to invest in society at this moment, it would greatly stimulate the economy and create untold thousands of jobs.

Evidence is solid that the 180 million Americans who don't smoke are demanding more and more that they be protected from smokers. Thank You For Not Smoking signs are sprouting up more and more in homes, offices, restaurants, cars, and public buildings. Lyndon Sanders started The Non-Smokers Inn in Dallas and is doing a land-office business. Thrifty Rent-A-Car has reserved a portion of its fleet for non-smokers only. Muse Airlines permits no smoking on its flights and their business is growing by leaps and bounds.

In all fairness to the youth of America I believe we have a moral obligation to teach, from the third grade upward (*many* fourth graders already smoke or have decided to smoke), that if they start smoking they will be unable to get jobs when they are sixteen.

Talking about jobs, Son, that's one of the reasons I'm delighted you do not smoke. I'm absolutely convinced that by 1987 the young man or woman smoker who enters the job market for the first time will be virtually unemployable. That's not an emotional statement, Son, but one that has been carefully thought out and discussed with employers and business leaders around the country from a financial point of view. In a nutshell, it just makes sense. Here's why.

Some 1981 figures (and they obviously will be substantially higher by 1987) are intriguing and frightening. To begin with, the smoker misses an average of 2.2 days per year more than the non-smoker because of illness. According to the most conservative of the conservative estimates, a smoker "steals" a minimum of thirty minutes a day from his employer to smoke (unless he's a pipe smoker, and then that figure is tripled). This does not include time away from his desk when he ostensibly is using the restroom, nor does it include the time when he is deep in thought (while he's inhaling, I might add) concerning his job. It's just plain time he steals to light up, smoke the cigarette, and put it out. This translates into an additional sixteen days a year *and* adversely affects his fellow employees by making them very resentful.

As an employer, Son, suppose I'm looking at two young men or women for employment. One smokes and the other doesn't. Since I know in advance that the non-smoker will give me an additional eighteen days of work per year, you tell me which one you think I (or any other informed employer) am going to hire.

Additionally, it requires seven times as much filtering equipment to clean the air in a room where smokers work as it does in a smoke-free room. (This does not include pipe or cigar smokers, because the air cannot be cleaned to acceptable levels where pipes or cigars are smoked.) Unless new technology is developed, the day will come when buildings will be built *not* to include smokers of any kind. The savings will be enormous.

It costs roughly six hundred dollars per year to clean up after a smoker—for filters, draperies, floors, wastebaskets, and ashtrays. Over five hundred dollars a year in burn damage is caused by the smoker who leaves or drops cigarettes on desks, credenzas, carpeting, sofas, and filing cabinets, as well as the occasional fire which often leads to loss of life. Health insurance premiums are substantially higher as a result of smokers. Additionally, the non-smoker who is working with smokers inhales the equivalent of from five to eleven cigarettes per day. We have no way of measuring how much productivity these workers lose because of the irritability factor.

The situation has reached the point, Son, where *The Wall Street Journal* published an article stating that many companies have on their application blanks at the top, "Do you smoke?" Underneath that question is the statement, "If the answer to the above is 'yes,' you need not bother to fill out the remaining portion of the application." This has been tested in the courts of California, and there's no legal problem because it does not discriminate because of race, creed, color, sex, or ethnic background. Smoking is an economic issue, a costly economic issue.

Look at it this way, Son. If two young men or women were applying to me for a job and one smoked and the other didn't, if everything else were equal—or even nearly equal—I could not justify paying one candidate over ninety dollars a week more than the other one. That's what it would cost me to hire the smoker instead of the non-smoker. We currently have approximately forty people on our payroll. If all of them smoked, it would cost me as an employer an additional $3,546 per week, which is well over $184,440 per year.

For thousands of small businesses the difference between operating at a profit or loss could well be the difference in hiring non-smokers instead of smokers. As a businessman I could never justify that additional expenditure for the "privilege" of hiring a smoker.

Glad you don't smoke, Son. Sure do love you.

DAD

Thought: *The term "smoker" is factually incorrect. The cigarette smokes and the person sucks on the cigarette. That makes him a* sucker.

WHAT WOULD *YOU* DO
WITH A BONUS?

Dear Family (and everybody else),

Well, you've gotten your first check from the family partnership, and I can understand some of your excitement. Any time something of an unexpected nature in the form of a financial bonanza takes place, it generates enthusiasm. With extra money you can clean up those nagging little bills and buy some of the extras you've been wanting. But girls, there's an inherent danger in such things.

When you think in terms of using a financial bonanza to pay bills created by overspending, indiscriminate buying, or even to indulge in a luxury spree, you are actually feeding the spending habit that got you into financial trouble in the first place.

As you probably know, the participants in the old "$64,000 Question" quiz show on television invariably ended up with less money five years later than they had before they won the big prize. The same situation is proving true also of the state lotteries. Even those who win several thousand dollars a month for X-number of years sometimes end up over-indulging and losing sight of basic values, which create other problems and are often disastrous. They've never been taught how to deal with that unexpected bonanza. Countless numbers of them have ended up with emotional difficulties, and others have had their entire families destroyed by fast living which often results in divorce.

Don't misunderstand, girls. When you have a bill, I would be terribly disappointed if you didn't pay it, but you should pay it out of the income you were earning when you acquired the debt. This builds character, and on character you can build a life.

When you receive an unexpected bonanza, one of the things you should do is set aside most of that money for an investment or savings program. You should deliberately plan a growth program instead of a catch-up program. Obviously, the money is yours and you can do with it as you will, but I'm hoping that you're making plans to use future funds in a growing way instead of a catching-up way.

Love,

DAD

P.S. *Perhaps I should have offered this advice when you received your checks, but I hesitated to do so for two reasons. First, you are all on your own and are responsible adults. In the truest sense of the word the money was yours. The decision as to how to use it was therefore yours. Second, I felt that regardless of whether you used the money wisely or unwisely, you would learn and benefit from*

the experience so that when the next check
comes your way it will be effectively used.

A SIMPLE INCIDENT

Dear Sweetnin' and every other child with an occasional rebellious tinge,

I suspect that you were too young to remember, but never will I forget what happened that day in the bathroom in Nashville, Tennessee. I was shaving when you walked in, opened the closet door, and pulled out the clothes basket. At that time you were about four years old, and I said to you, "Put the basket back in the closet, Cindy." You looked up at me and said, "No."

I'll have to confess I was pretty shocked, but I quickly regained my composure and said, "Yes, you will, too!" Again you said, "No." This was direct rebellion and disobedience I could not tolerate from my beautiful little girl. I picked you up, lightly warmed your bottom, set you back down, and said, "Now you put the basket back in the closet." You defiantly said "No." Again I picked you up and this time I warmed your bottom more firmly, put you down, and said, "Now, you put it back in the closet." With tears in your eyes and your lips quivering you again looked at me and defiantly said, "No."

To tell you the truth, Sweetnin', I was beginning to wish I had never raised the issue, but I hope you understand what I say when I point out that I could not let you win. I felt my authority was being questioned, and I knew if I lost at this point to a four-year-old that we both would be in trouble when you got older. So, for the third time I picked you up, spanked you, and again instructed you to put the basket back in the closet. Since at that time I outweighed you by nearly two hundred pounds, you apparently decided it would be wise to go ahead and put the basket back in the closet.

I've thought about that incident many times, Sweetnin', and I'm convinced it is one of those things that made a difference in both our lives. At any rate, I just wanted to let you know that I hated to have to spank you, but I loved you too much not to. Sure do love you, Baby.

DAD

Thought: *Psychologist James Dobson says that discipline is something you do* for *a child. Punishment is something you do* to *a child.*

Note: *For those who don't believe in physical discipline, I offer this thought: It is Scripturally sound. I'm obviously not talking about "beating" a child. Twenty minutes after the third spanking there was no sign of rebellion or defiance. As a matter of fact, she was more loving than ever.*

PRIDE GOETH BEFORE A FALL

Dear Tom (and everybody else),

What a day! We were running a little late for school and you wanted to stop by one of the local fast-food stands and get their sandwich breakfast to eat on the way. We ordered the breakfast, but when I pulled up to the window, I realized I had left my money at home. I didn't see that as too big a problem because I had frequently spoken for this company and felt they would know me.

The ensuing conversation took place: "Good morning, I'm Zig Ziglar. Do you recognize my name?" Manager: "No." Zig: "I speak at conventions, I've written a couple of books, and I've spoken for your company on numerous occasions. Does the name still not ring a bell?" Manager: "No, it doesn't." Zig: "Here's my problem. I left my money at home and I just ordered my son a breakfast. Could I possibly bring the money back after I take him to school?" Manager: "If you will leave your watch as security." Zig: "Forget it."

With that, Son, I'm embarrassed to say that I left. As I drove off, you let me have it right between my eyes! "Dad, you came across as proud, arrogant, and egotistical." With a little irritation and shock, I responded, "Well, Son, I might have, but I didn't think I was that bad!"

Of course, I didn't feel that I had behaved that badly because I was looking at it through my own, highly prejudiced eyes. At any rate, Son, pride, arrogance, and egotism are terrible burdens for an individual to carry. Fortunately, they can be corrected, and I just wanted you to know that your observation that day made me more aware of the fact that I need to be extremely careful in this area. I'm sorry I embarrassed you, Son. I'll try to be a better role model in the future.

Love,

DAD

ARE HOMOSEXUALS "BORN THAT WAY"?

Dear Hoss,

Over the years you and I have talked about every subject under the sun, but in the last two or three years we have had many talks about homosexuals and homosexuality. In the past three or four years I have probably read over two thousand pages on the subject, not counting many newspaper and magazine articles. Many people, including you, have asked questions on the subject, and since there is a combination of fear, ignorance, misinformation, and apathy regarding homosexuality, I felt I needed to address the subject and give our family and our readers some basic information. Additionally, I include sources of information that will give hope, help, and encouragement to those individuals who have been caught in the homosexual trap and want out.

I believe the information is timely because recently in Dallas there was considerable excitement in the homosexual community. The laws prohibiting sodomy had been stricken down and homosexuals in Texas and all over the country hailed the decision. In many people's minds, including my own, there was considerable dismay at the reversal. My mind continues to go back to about six years ago when I was speaking in Buffalo, New York. At the break a man of sixty-five came to talk with me. In all of my life I have never seen such sad eyes. He said, "I need to talk to you." With this he handed me a note and walked away.

Before the next break I had a chance to read the note, and during the break he and I had a chance to talk. His story is one that is repeated often in our society today. When he was ten years old he told his parents that he thought he was a homosexual. It seems that his parents were "enlightened," and so they said to him, "Son, we love you regardless, and whatever makes you happy is what we want for you."

He looked at me and said, "For fifty years I was a practicing homosexual. Five years ago I committed my life to Christ and came out of homosexuality, but it hasn't been easy. When I think of the family and children I could have had and the grandchildren I could now be enjoying, it's almost more than I can bear." I'll never forget the look in his eyes as he turned and walked away.

As I address this subject I emphasize that my first concern is for those homosexuals who, as children, were inducted into the homosexual lifestyle via incest, seduction, rape, or by an older homosexual. Tragically, many of them feel — primarily because of erroneous information about homosexuality — that they are stuck with their condition. Not true. Personal experience with those who have come out of homosexuality, scientific information available to any concerned reader, and Scriptural reading prove this point.

I also have great concern and compassion for the families of practicing homosexuals who are under intense pressure to love them as they are instead of loving them enough to pray and counsel with them to help them come out of homosexuality.

There is considerable controversy concerning homosexuality, but as far as I'm concerned anyone who has the scientific and Scriptural information available today would have to admit that the practice of homosexuality is a sin and that they were not "born that way." Let me express my feelings, and I do so because I believe an objective viewpoint is needed. In our own family we have dozens of grandchildren, nieces, nephews, and cousins. In America we have millions of children whose very lives depend on an informed *and* aroused citizenry. My Christian background will cause me to speak from that perspective, but I believe it is objective because I have read both sides of the issue in considerable detail.

Homosexuals say they were "born that way," that if they'd had any choice in the matter, they would never have gone that route. The reason I know this cannot be true is very simple. In the Book of Leviticus God says that homosexuality is a sin unto death (Lev. 20:13). The God I love and worship would never make a person a homosexual and then kill him for being one. It just doesn't make any sense.

The second factor is the physiological nature of mankind. It's obvious that men and women are rather dramatically different and that each has a specific purpose in the creative process of life. Homosexuals contend that they do not "recruit" others to be homosexuals. Obviously if they did not recruit them, then after a period of time homosexuality would no longer exist because they are parasitic and do not reproduce. Without recruitment, homosexuality would disappear.

Number three, the Masters and Johnson study covering sixteen years revealed that over 60 percent of the homosexuals who want to rid themselves of homosexuality can do so with the aid of counseling. The doctors use only scientific information and do not use Scriptural support. I'm confident the figure would be substantially higher with God in the picture.

The *Kinsey Report*, which homosexuals frequently quote, revealed that 10 percent of American males practice homosexuality for about three years between the ages of eleven and fifty-five and then stop. As a practical matter, can you conceive of a heterosexual being "counseled" out of feeling attracted to a member of the opposite sex? Personally, when I look at that Redhead of mine I know you could counsel me for four thousand years and you could never talk me out of loving her as my wife. My affection for her, my feeling toward the opposite sex, is not open to counseling; it's a fact of life.

Fourth point: statistical data is substantial that in certain environments homosexuality flourishes. In homes where there is a brutal, domineering, unloving father, the incidence is much higher than usual. In homes where there is an absentee father, combined with a "smother mother," the incidence is much higher. If homosexuals were "born that way," why does the environment contribute to their being homosexuals?

Fifth point: In South American countries where fathers and sons, as well as brothers and cousins — in short, members of the male sex — are openly affectionate with each other, the incidence of homosexuality is virtually unknown. Again, why would that situation prevail?

Sixth point: Identical twins whose genes and chromosomes are the same have been separated at birth and raised under different circumstances. Documented cases reveal that on occasion one was heterosexual and the other a practicing homosexual.

Another reason I include this letter in this book is because of the social acceptance of homosexuality, combined with sex education, which often describes homosexuality as simply an "acceptable alternate lifestyle." Combine this with the increasing role of Planned Parenthood, which is essentially humanistic, and I believe you will share in my deep concern. As the Baron de Tocqueville said when he toured America in the 1830s, "America is great because America is good. If America ever ceases to be good, America will cease to be great."

One of the incredible ironies of homosexual thinking was evidenced during a recent homosexual demonstration celebrating the first anniversary of the repeal of the sodomy law in Texas. Demonstrators wore buttons proclaiming, "Gay Is Healthy," while carrying signs demanding that the Federal government appropriate 100 million dollars to fight homosexual disease. *Every* time homosexuality is mentioned in God's Word it is condemned, and Romans 1:27 is quite clear that the homosexual today is reaping the seeds of his deviant lifestyle.

As you probably know, Americans are finally responding to the charge that the heterosexual's "irrational" behavior and ostracism of homosexuals is based on fear and ignorance. There is some fear, but it is based on solid, documented facts that should concern every heterosexual American. Example: Homosexuals and bisexuals combined make up less than 5 percent of the population but account for 44 percent of all male syphilis, 51 percent of all gonorrhea of the throat, 35 percent of all hepatitis B, and 53 percent of all enteric disease! (Dr. Paul Cameron, possibly the best informed man in America on the subject, challenges anyone to show him *one* 25-year-old male homosexual who does not have or has not had at least one venereal disease.)

As the average American's awareness of what homosexuals do in a sexual encounter increases, the rejection of the homosexual lifestyle will increase. Surely no one who understands what happens in a homosexual bath (two to twenty sexual encounters in a single night!) or what "hand balling," "rimming," or "golden showers" involve would seriously consider homosexuality either "normal," "loving," or socially acceptable.

In a real sense, Hoss, you and I are involved in homosexuality because what homosexuals do has an impact on me, you, and everyone else. I say that for the very simple reason that in our society the incidence of venereal disease, especially Herpes, is rampant in the homosexual community. Infectious hepatitis is roughly ten times as prevalent in the homosexual community as elsewhere. The *always*-fatal AIDS (Acquired Immune Deficiency Syndrome) exists primarily in the homosexual community and is doubling roughly every six months. It has no known cure, and a victim can have the disease for as long as two years before it surfaces. Medical evidence is solid that it is transmitted by sexual contact, and the exchange of body fluids such as blood, semen, and possibly saliva.

At this time AIDS, hepatitis, and many venereal diseases are spreading like wildfire, thanks to a large degree to the 250 to 500 sexual contacts many homosexuals have in a single year. Yes, my brother, we are involved, as is every American who has a blood transfusion or who eats in a restaurant where homosexuals are employed.

Additionally, 50 percent of the homosexuals admit to having sex outdoors; 41 percent in public bathrooms; and 34 percent in bars. That is lust, not love, and is the reason God *always* speaks of homosexual lust and *never* speaks of homosexual love.

At this time homosexuals are the best organized and possibly have more media clout than any other group in the country. For example, any program dealing with homosexuals must be cleared through the homosexual consultant hired and paid for by each television network (according to *TV Guide*). Can you imagine the networks giving Christians or *any* other group the same opportunity to make certain our story is fairly told?

Despite homosexuals' favorable publicity and media clout, the overwhelming majority of Americans do not approve of homosexuals and their lifestyle. For example, a survey conducted in America's one hundred largest newspapers nationwide produced 723,300 responses to the question, "Do you approve of known practicing homosexuals teaching in public schools?" Only 33,600 said yes, while 689,700 said "no." Percentage-wise, that's 95.4 percent opposed versus 4.6 percent in favor. Question: Is that response based on irrational fear, or is it because 79 percent of the cases of recorded teacher-pupil sex is homosexual?

From a moral point of view, the documentation *is* overwhelming that the number of sexual contacts by homosexuals greatly exceeds that of the heterosexual, running in many instances to as many as twenty thousand contacts in a lifetime. That is not a moral approach to life. It's total lust.

Then there's the happiness factor. The rate of alcoholism among homosexuals is substantially higher than it is among heterosexuals and the murder rate is dramatically higher in the homosexual community.

To the best of my knowledge, most mass murders committed in the last twenty years that were spread over a period of time (meaning simply that somebody did not go berserk and walk into a tavern and start shooting) were homosexual-related: Juan Corona in California, Wayne Williams in Atlanta, Wayne Henley in Houston, Jim Jones (bisexual) in Guyana, and the Gacy case in Gary, Indiana. No wonder less than 2 percent of the homosexuals who describe themselves as "gay" would want a son of theirs to be homosexual.

I include this information as a warning because as social acceptance of homosexuality grows, the temptation to experiment will grow. Many young men and women have decided to experiment, had one or two experiences, and then felt they were unworthy of love from a member of the opposite sex. As a result, they have continued to participate in homosexuality.

Along these lines I would like to offer a thought on the Christian approach to dealing with the homosexual. We've certainly been in error on this one. Many times as Christians we piously adjust our halos and say, "The homosexual act is a sin. Quit it, and then come join our church." Interestingly enough, we will say to the rapist, thief, drug addict, murderer, and other sinners, "Come and accept Christ as Lord and He will clean your life," but we are saying to the homosexual, "Clean up your life. *Then* we'll welcome you into the church."

We should first welcome them into the church, making it crystal clear that anyone who continues to rob, steal, kill, rape, commit adultery, *or* practice homosexuality is sinning, and in the eyes of God that is not acceptable. We should follow the same procedure Christ follows. He hates the sin but He loves the sinner, so He takes *all* of us sinners as we are. *Then* He works the changes in our lives.

Love,

Zig

Note: *I urge parents who have a son or daughter who is practicing homosexuality to become knowledgeable on the subject. Continue to love your child, but* don't give him up *to the practice of homosexuality. Read:* Gay Is Not Good, *by Dr. Frank M. DeMas;* The Gospel and the Gay, *by Kenneth O. Gangel; and* Growing Up Straight, *by Wyden and Wyden.*

Fact: *British anthropologist Dr. John D. Unwin, in a study involving eighty civilizations covering a span of four thousand years, proved beyond any reasonable doubt that each of these civilizations fell within one generation after the family collapsed. In most — if not all — of these cases, the final step in the destruction of the family was the acceptance and impact of homosexuality.*
I include this information in our family book for two reasons: First, I'm deeply concerned that America is in serious moral trouble and homosexuality is the bottom rung of the moral ladder. Second, I firmly believe that when the American public is educated on homosexuality (the books suggested in this letter would provide an excellent base), a significant step will have been taken toward solving the problem.

LEAD WITH
YOUR HEART

Dear Family,

Over the years each of you has discussed the many facets of success with me. In a thousand different ways you've wanted to know how to succeed in life and what is necessary to be successful. This example doesn't answer all of that question, but it is an answer to part of it.

My good friend, Dr. Richard Furman from Boone, North Carolina, wrote a beautiful book entitled, *To Be a Surgeon.* During one of our visits, Dr. Furman gave me a pacemaker which had been rejected by the manufacturer. He explained that this particular one would probably work 9,999 times out of 10,000, but that it may malfunction the 10,000th time. He explained that human life was far too precious for them to gamble on a pacemaker that only worked 9,999 times out of 10,000.

The pacemaker is a device about the size of a cigarette lighter. When it is operating full force, the electrical impulse is so slight that the average person cannot feel it if he is holding it in his bare hands. The skin is just too tough. However, when the surgeons insert the pacemaker underneath the skin and connect it to a small wire that is passed into the heart, the heart is so sensitive that it picks up the minute electrical impulses and the life-sustaining function of the heart is regulated by the pacemaker.

Yes, the heart is very sensitive. It is my conviction that most people miss success and happiness by about ten inches, which is the distance from the head to the heart. Unfortunately, too many of us are like calloused skin rather than a sensitive heart. With this in mind, I make every effort when I speak or write to communicate from my head *and* my heart to the heads and hearts of the people who hear me speak or read what I write.

My greatest concern and my primary prayers are directed at the *hearts* of my reading and listening audiences. The reason is simple. If a person isn't convicted in his heart, then his involvement and effectiveness will be minimal. A high-jumper broke a world's record and somebody asked him how he was able to do it. His reply: "I threw my heart over the bar and the rest of me followed."

Love,

DAD

Point: *If you want to achieve the success you are capable of achieving, whether it's in academics, athletics, business, family, or your relationship with Jesus Christ, put your heart into the venture and the rest of you will follow.*

WORDS CAN
—AND *DO*—
MAKE A DIFFERENCE

Dear Family,

I've always been concerned about the words we use in our everyday conversation. Words reveal what is inside of us. They're powerful.

As you know, God spoke and the world appeared. Over eleven hundred times in His Bible He talks about words. In my own life I spoke some words in love and acquired my lifetime mate. I said some words in faith and assured myself of an eternity with Jesus Christ.

It is an absolute fact that words can either encourage or destroy a person. That's one of the reasons we never permitted the use of negative words, put-downs, vulgarity, or profanity. Words paint pictures, and when those negative or "nasty" words enter the subconscious mind they create all kinds of problems. I'm appalled by the people who casually, arrogantly, or thoughtlessly take God's name in vain. I shudder to think about the consequences of regularly breaking one of the Ten Commandments.

Yes, words are so important. "You can do it" can make a difference in a discouraged person's life. "That was a beautiful job. Your room looks so neat!" "Sweetheart, I really loved that dinner. I believe that's the best salad you've ever made, and the roast was out of this world." "My, how pretty you are today, and how good you smell!" "I love you so much." And the list goes on.

Yes, Family, we believe in using the right words in our household. Encouraging words are important, but they must be sincere or they become little white lies and lose their effectiveness. I encourage you to spread the good words because words can give hope and encouragement and, goodness knows, in our world today we certainly need lots of encouragement.

Love,

DAD

YOU CAN MAKE
A DIFFERENCE

Dear Ziglar Children (and everybody else),

One of the saddest things in our society today is the feeling among so many people that what they do can't really make any difference. They seem to feel that one person doesn't matter, especially if that person happens to be they. Well, as you know, kids, I believe that one person can make an incredible difference. We never know what the impact of an individual will be on another person's life or, for that matter, thousands of people's lives.

I think of Anne Sullivan, who taught and inspired Helen Keller. Anne herself was helped by an elderly nurse who looked at her and saw potential for what she could *do* rather than her mental condition at the moment. I don't think anyone would question the fact that Helen Keller positively affected millions of lives. Yet, without Anne Sullivan, and before her, without the influence of that elderly nurse, Helen Keller would never have had her chance in life. It's a fact that someone taught Albert Einstein that two times two equals four, and someone else taught Beethoven the musical scale. Just think of the lives these people influenced!

General Motors started in the mind of one man. Ford Motor Company started in the mind of one man. So did DuPont. Tupperware started in the mind of one woman, as did Home Interiors and Gifts and Mary Kay Cosmetics. As a matter of fact, all companies start in the mind of one person.

So, kids, all of this to say that when you have a conviction about something, your efforts and belief in that one thing can substantially influence the lives of millions of people. I think of Madalyn Murray O'Hair who, in my mind, is one of the saddest people on this earth. Yet, through her efforts prayer was taken out of the public schools.

The point is obvious. One person can do a tremendous amount of good or a tremendous amount of harm. But the point is the same: one person can make a dramatic difference. Each *one* of you is *one* person and, yes, *you* can and will make a difference. My faith tells me that you are going to make it a positive difference—not in just one life, but in many lives. Chances are good that something you say or do *today* will positively *or* negatively affect someone you know and perhaps love. *Don't take any chances.* Make it a positive influence. Everybody wins when you do what is right.

Love,

DAD

THE FUTURE BELONGS
TO THOSE WHO
PREPARE FOR IT

Dear Family (and everybody else),

One of the most traumatic events in recent history, as far as the city of Dallas is concerned, was the bankruptcy and demise of Braniff International. A number of my friends lost their jobs after many, many years of employment. This morning I caught a few minutes of the local news about a former executive who had lost his job with another company after working with them for years. He is now in pretty serious financial difficulty. This reminded me again that life is uncertain and that we should do some planning for the future. God tells us repeatedly that willful waste makes woeful want.

Those exact words are from your grandmother, but they also are an admonition from God.

I'm certain you remember the story of Joseph and the Pharoah—how God warned Joseph in a dream that seven years of plenty would be followed by seven years of famine, and that they should prepare for the famine during the years of plenty. That's the advice I would like to pass on to you today. At the moment all of you are gainfully employed. You might not have a surplus of money in the bank, but by most standards you are comfortable. By over 90 percent of the world's standards you are wealthy.

The major purpose of this letter is to urge each one of you to embark upon a systematic procedure of preparing for your future by putting at least 10 percent of your monthly income into gilt-edged securities or the money market, so that you can be ready if a rare business opportunity comes your way. A nest egg is also handy if you have any reversals or an emergency over which you have no control.

Incidentally, I encourage the people at our company to do the same thing, even though we have many built-in benefits such as profit-sharing and a pension-trust plan that will take care of many of their needs in the future. Realistically, none of us has a crystal ball focused on the future. Inflation might make such serious inroads into those profit-sharing and pension trust funds that our people might need additional funds.

This message is simple. Don't spend everything you have. If there is a surplus, instead of putting it into luxuries lay aside a portion of *everything* for your future. Remember, the future belongs to those who prepare for it.

Love,

DAD

GOLF IS CHARACTER-BUILDING AND CHARACTER-REVEALING

Dear Tom (and all other golfers),

It was another one of those red-letter days, Son. As you remember, we were on the fourth hole on the golf course at Brookhaven Country Club. You put your third shot into the trap, and I put my second shot slightly over the trap and to the left of the green. At the time you were only ten years old.

As I was addressing my ball after walking past you, I looked up and saw your ball fly out of the trap and stop next to the pin for almost a "gimme." I was elated when you sank your putt for a bogey on a tough par four. I congratulated you on a beautiful sand shot, but you looked at me and said, "Dad, that was my second shot. I missed the first one in the sand trap." Then you paused for a moment and said, "You know, Dad, I started not to tell you about missing the first one. But then I realized it was Satan who was trying to influence me, and I told him to get out of the way, that what he wanted me to do wasn't right."

How proud I was of you, Son. Learning moral values is the most important part of your education, and the fact that at age ten you recognized Satan would try to influence you is a sign of significant spiritual maturity. Just remember that Christ has already defeated him and that you and Christ can continue to defeat him. That will put you a full step ahead of most people. This won't just set you apart from the crowd, Son. It will set you above.

Love,

DAD

Fact: *If you lie, cheat, or steal in little things, the inevitable result, given enough time, is that you will lie, cheat, and steal in the big things. There is no little white lie. The cancer of corruption is hidden in all of them.*

Dear Reader,

Recently I received some correspondence from a friend of mine, Thomas G. Kamp, who is vice-chairman of the Business & Technology Cooperative Ventures for Control Data. The correspondence included the academic record of his son Tom, a copy of a newspaper clipping enumerating the awards Tom Kamp had earned during his four years at Southern Methodist University, and a copy of a letter Tom had written to his dad.

Upon entering the School of Engineering, Tom had set a goal of scoring a perfect 4.0 grade average. He accomplished that objective and graduated summa cum laude. He was named recipient of the 1982–83 university award for outstanding scholar of his graduating class. He was inducted into numerous honorary societies and is the recipient of the Austin Merit Scholarship from the Northwestern University Graduate School of Management. During his academic career Tom also pursued his interest in flying and served as the secretary for a Bible study group.

This outstanding young man spells out in his letter to his dad and in his speech the reasons for his amazing accomplishments. They are so beautiful and significant that I, along with Mr. Kamp, wanted you to share the true secrets of success from a remarkable young man.

First, let's look at the letter from Tom to his dad.

May 8, 1983

Dad,

Here's a copy of my speech. I dreamt about giving this speech long
before I was ever asked to give it. Contained in this speech are the *two
secrets* (see speech) of my success. You taught me both secrets, Dad.
Thanks for giving me so much of an education outside of school and
for all the opportunities for personal growth. You have consistently
been proud of me. I hope that I will live my life in a way that you can
continue to be proud.

Love,

Tommy

I know you'll agree it's a beautiful letter from a young man to
his dad. His speech, when he received the award for outstanding scholar, says a great deal more.

I'd like to say a sincere "thank you" to you, Mr. Provost, for this
award and to all the faculty members for their support. I have called
upon you, my professors, countless times for some extra help or
instruction outside of class. Sometimes it was tough to get in touch
with you, but once I contacted you, I was always treated courteously
and professionally. I've asked favors of men such as Dr. Petty in
philosophy and Dr. Baughn in engineering, and they were more
than willing to help out. I've asked advice of men such as Dr. Pack-
man and it was freely given. I respect and admire so many of you, the
SMU faculty. Therefore, it is a momentous experience to receive
your respect and recognition symbolized by this award.

Here I am, graduating very near the top of my class from SMU.
What was my secret for doing so well?

As a freshman I came to SMU like most other students, I guess. I
was excited about "being out on my own" and away from home, but
yet a little nervous for the very same reasons. I went to a high school
that gave me a great foundation to build on. But there are many
people from my high school who haven't done very well, so that
couldn't be the main cause of my success.

The secret of my success goes back farther than high school. It goes
back to the person who I respect and admire more than any other.
That person is my father. His life has always been exemplary. It is

this man, my father, who taught me the secret. In a word, the secret is "dedication."

Your presence here tonight at this honorary dinner indicates that you also understand the secret of dedication. Dedication is a constant attention to the details of one's work. Dedication is long-term oriented. It doesn't expect a result in the short term. Anyone can stop trying after working a problem and getting the wrong answer or no answer at all; the dedicated person keeps trying and trying until he or she does get the right answer by the right method. I don't particularly enjoy studying and I don't think any of you do either. Yet those of us who are dedicated arrange our priorities so that our work consistently comes before pleasure. Many Friday and Saturday nights are spent with a cold, hard, dull textbook while our friends are out on the town having the times of their lives. The fruits of our dedication here at SMU are now ripe and ready to be picked. Those of us who want to pursue further study have been accepted by the best graduate schools, law schools, or med schools. Those of us who want to start work have a host of job offers to choose from. Some of our friends who have been partying for the past four years do not have any job offers at all. Thomas Henry Huxley may have said it best when he wrote: "Perhaps the most valuable result of all education is the ability to make yourself do the thing you have to do, when it ought to be done, whether you like it or not; it is the first lesson that ought to be learned; ... "

Although I am dedicated, it would be inappropriate for me to not give credit to the person who made it possible for me to receive this award. I would like to inform you that I didn't do all my work alone. I received help on every assignment. I was aided every time I studied. I was not 100 percent honest when I signed my name below the words: "On my honor, I have neither given nor received aid on this work." I have indeed received help on every test I've taken.

Before you call the Honor Council, please allow me to explain. I received help from God. Does that surprise you? It shouldn't. God is the source of all wisdom and knowledge. God organizes my mind every time I study. He helps me recall information on tests. He also does much, much more for me than help me in academics. It is to Him that I would like the praise and honor to go.

In conclusion, I would like to say that SMU and its outstanding faculty members have indeed performed their duty. The graduating class of 1983 is quite different from the entering class of fall 1979. We may have the same I.D. numbers, but our minds have changed. Our horizons have broadened. We have matured. We have learned new ways to analyze the problems of today. SMU and its faculty members have performed this education. "The great end of education," as Tyron Edwards once said, "is to discipline rather than to furnish the mind; to train it to use of its own powers, rather than fill it with the accumulations of others."

Thank you.

When you sum it up, that's really what life's all about. Tom Kamp had the advantage of being from a beautiful and loving home and having parents who guided him in many areas of life. He also had the enormous advantage of having committed his life to Christ. Additionally, here is a young man who, as he indicated in his speech, had worked very hard and had dedicated himself to using his ability.

The message speaks volumes. When loving parents teach children strong moral values (faith, discipline, dedication, and hard work), they *can* resist the strong peer pressure to live it up and be one of the gang. The message is beautiful and should be encouraging to all of us.

Sincerely,

ZIG ZIGLAR

WELCOME, AND
WATCH OUT—
THIS IS COLLEGE

Dear Tom, and all other college freshmen,

For years your mother and I have heard comments about the "empty nest." It's hard to believe our little boy is now a young man in college, but fortunately, and unfortunately, your mother and I now know the feeling of that empty nest. Fortunately,

Son, because it's a sign of your growth toward manhood. What a tragedy it would be if you remained forever a child and under our care. Yet it is unfortunate for us because our last one is gone and there is an emptiness around the house.

Your call Monday evening preceded this letter I had intended to write earlier. I wanted to share with you some thoughts about college life and some of the situations you will encounter. You and I have talked about many things, but your phone call alerted me to one I had not contemplated, namely, your first encounter with a cult group.

This group, like many others, has discovered part of the truth and honestly believes they are the only ones with a chance to make it through those Pearly Gates. Fortunately, I was at least partially familiar with them, so we could intelligently chat about a couple of the fallacies of their belief. Even more fortunately, Son, and for this I'm eternally grateful, your own faith and Scriptural knowledge is solid, and consequently you were largely prepared to deal with the situation yourself.

A word of caution. Many of the cult groups are totally sincere, and most are committed to winning converts to their beliefs. To accomplish this objective they will go to incredible lengths, including subterfuge, brainwashing, coercion, and downright misrepresentation.

Generally speaking, the cults are built around the personality of one individual, either living or dead, who claimed some kind of divine guidance for his "insights." Fortunately, Son, the Bible deals extensively with this very subject, and we're encouraged to handle members of the cults according to the Scripture. We find this in numerous passages: Romans 16:17; Galatians 1:6–9; I Timothy 4:1–3; II Timothy 4:3,4; Titus 3:10; II Peter 2:1; and Jude 19.

Since you've already had two encounters and have graciously received them and clearly stated your position, I believe you have established what you believe and your total absence of interest in their false doctrine. You now need to be on the alert to the fact that they will possibly make other efforts to show you that they are "nice people," which they probably are—only misguided people. I don't question their sincerity, but you can be sincere and wrong. Keep this in mind, Son, as they try to win your friendship and encourage you to partici-pate in some of their social events.

One thing you will notice is that cults have great single-ness of purpose, which is an admirable characteristic if the purpose is God-centered and based entirely on God's Book. Unfortunately, theirs is man-centered and based on half-truths.

When you encounter individuals like this and the situa-tion is such that you must spend time with them, just remem-ber there is much you can do to protect yourself and your faith. First, you can ask God to give you wisdom, love, and discernment so you will recognize truth. Second, you can pray for that individual. Third, you can keep the communica-tion lines open with Mom and Dad so we can address the issues head-on as they arise. Fourth, you can meet, as you have already done this year, with some of the theologians at our church and Bible institute who love God and are deeply committed to their belief that the Bible is God's Word and is without error. These men can and will help you find the Godly answers you need.

There are some other individuals you need to be aware of. These are the "intellectuals" who delight in finding fault and challenging the validity of your faith. You might find them in the dorm, in the classroom, or even at the church. On the surface they often appear to be cool, laid-back individuals who have it all together. All you really need to do, Son, is check their peace of mind and the real joy they get out of life. In these two departments they just don't have what you have.

The early days of your college education are important, and your indoctrination into college life has certainly been swift. Within thirty-six hours of your arrival you've already had three significant experiences. First, the young man who sold you and your roommate the elevator passes, when, in fact, your dormitory has no elevators, was a typical college prank. They've been doing that at your college for generations and since only two dollars was involved, it was an inexpensive lesson for a trusting—perhaps even gullible—twosome. For two dollars you learned that everything in life is not exactly as it seems. You and your roommate were both good-natured about it and are already planning to recoup the two dollars when the next group of freshmen comes in.

Your second exposure was with a cult, and we've dealt with that. The third one was, unfortunately, one of those things that many young men and women seem to think is a natural part of life. I speak of the beer party that took place the first night. I was delighted to know that you felt totally out of place at the get-together, which you were led to believe was a mandatory occasion. I'm also glad you witnessed the more unpleasant side of those "marvelously fun" get-togethers. As you reported, one of the boys threw up in the hallway and another on the stairway. Somehow that didn't strike you as being fun.

You will see a lot of that, Son, during your four years. But we've talked about drinking all our lives and I know exactly how you feel and you know how your mother and I feel, so we're not concerned that you will participate, even casually. You have gone to college to continue your education and I'm delighted that you clearly understand that what Henry Ford said is true: "Education is not something to prepare you for life. It is a continuous part of life." It's simply another step in the never-ending quest for growth and knowledge.

The first few days and weeks of your college life are the most important. During this period you will establish the habits that will insure excellent academic achievement and establish winning social relationships, or you will acquire habits and establish relationships that will have a negative impact. The choice, and the results that follow, will be yours.

Your sleep, study, and exercise habits will be formed early. Every evening, Son, if you will simply jot down your activities for that day in your Goal Planner (it will take no more than five minutes), it will enable you to keep your attention focused on the truly important things.

As you know, it's easy to get into the habit of sleeping a few more minutes, and then having to make the mad dash for the first class, often arriving late and occasionally missing significant points or assignments. It's easy to get into the habit of joining too many bull sessions about unimportant subjects. Don't misunderstand. Part of the excitement and benefit of college is making those friends who will have lifelong impacts. The only thing, Son, is that balance is so important, and many of the bull sessions go nowhere and accomplish absolutely nothing. I simply urge you to be careful with your time and the people with whom you're involved.

One of the good things about college is that you will have a chance to see what kind of money manager you are. James Moffatt expressed it well. He said that a man's treatment of money—how he makes it and how he spends it—is *the* most decisive test of his character. My first employer always told me that if a man couldn't save a little money when he was making a little, he'd never be able to save a lot when he was making a lot. I have found that to be an accurate observation, Son, and with this in mind I encourage you to take your weekly stipend and use it carefully.

You start with your tithing habit, because ten percent of the money is God's. As a matter of fact, all of it is God's. You honor Him and maintain the discipline you've maintained all your life. You don't even think about tithing. You simply tithe and God will honor you for it. We've talked a great deal about money and goals in other parts of the book, but I wanted to make one more statement concerning money in the context of habits and college life.

One of the really nice things about your college is the fact that you're close enough so that we're available if needed, and yet far enough away so that you're definitely on your own. We've already talked about the trips back and forth, and I am going to remind you strongly that you've agreed to drive within the speed limit. The law says fifty-five, and you, Dad, and everybody else should abide by it.

When your study load is not heavy and you finish classes at noon, the temptation to hop in your car and drive the sixty miles to Dallas can be overwhelming. I know you're going to be tempted, but I'm hoping you are disciplined and mature enough to say "no" to that whim. You're probably going to be home every weekend, and there are many things you need to be doing during those afternoon and evening hours. Since you're determined to play good golf and make a contribution to the golf team, you should spend any extra time learning how to hit that golf ball better. While you're at it, pick up some extra tips for old Dad so he can do the same thing!

Of course, there's also the fact that while you might be doing well in all your classes, the chances are pretty good that you're not learning all there is to know about the subject, so spend those extra hours really digging in and becoming better informed. Additionally, you have excellent gym facilities to start whipping your body into the kind of shape that will enable it to serve you all of your life and make you a better golfer in the process.

In conclusion, Son, I guess one of the reasons for this letter is that I have found it very difficult to perform the operation my friend, Psychologist Denis Waitley, says is necessary for all parents and their children. It's called a "parentectomy," and it separates the parent and the child. Chances are good we will never totally complete that operation, even though you are now largely on your own and soon will be completely on your own. As your parents we will always have a deep interest in everything you do and look forward to visits and conferences all our lives.

As you know, our love for you is unconditional. It has nothing to do with what you are and your own personal behavior. For the record, we are extremely proud of you — your moral values, your spiritual commitments, *and* your personal behavior. We now look forward to the preparation stage, getting you ready to go into life on your own. I'm confident we will be proud of you as your make your contributions.

Love,

DAD

Part IV

COURTSHIP, LOVE, MARRIAGE, AND SEX

Dear Reader,

Many times when we look at a project that is nearing completion, the natural tendency is to overlook or be unaware of the time and effort that has gone into the project. This is certainly true of marriage. Today many people, including family, friends, and strangers, comment on the beautiful relationship my wife and I enjoy. Our relationship, however, hasn't always been this beautiful. We've had our share of differences and difficulties, as the next three letters indicate. Three things are significant. Number one: We love each other and have always felt we could work out our problems. Number two: We both came from Christian homes and had been taught that marriage was permanent, so we *never* considered divorce. Number three: In July of 1972, I committed my life to Jesus Christ and at that point a good marriage became a truly great marriage.

ZIG ZIGLAR

SOME MEN ARE BOYS
WHEN THEY
GET MARRIED

Dear Sugar Babe, and other girls married to less-than-grown-up men,

As you remember, we had more arguments over petty little nothings during the first twelve months of our marriage than we had for the next thirty-six years. In retrospect, I believe that I was a pretty tough guy to live with. Aren't we fortunate to have had mothers who taught us that marriage was a permanent agreement? I was doubly fortunate to find the girl who loved me enough to patiently wait for me to grow up and out of some of my immature—even childish—behavior. Had you been an ordinary girl you would have gone home to Mama because of a series of incidents that individually were no big deal, but collectively were pretty heavy.

Do you remember the first time we ate out after we had returned from our honeymoon? As my new bride, you had been cooking three big meals every day and you needed a break. I begrudgingly, defiantly agreed to take you out to dinner. Then I proceeded to punish you with my attitude and complete lack of concern for your feelings. What a miserable evening I made out of that one!

To be honest, Sugar Babe, I don't know how you survived those early years. Marriage is a lot more fun now that we are more considerate of each other's needs and wishes. You're just a fun girl to be married to!

Your ever-lovin' husband,

HILARY

Thought: *When you argue and disagree over little things,* don't *follow the example I set in this letter.* Do *make up after* little *differences and it will, as I finally learned, make a* big *difference in your marriage.*

LITTLE THINGS
OFTEN MAKE
—OR BREAK—
A MARRIAGE

Dear Sugar Baby,

It happened thirty-six years ago, but I'll bet you remember it. We'd been married only a few months, and I'm embarrassed to say that as a young husband I wanted you at my beck and call every moment. After all, you were *my* wife and the minister had said, " 'Til death do us part."

Remember that little apartment we had just settled into when you decided to go home to visit your folks? You had been gone about a week and I expected you to arrive back in Columbia, South Carolina, where I was attending the university, in a matter of about two hours. Then I got a telephone call. You were on the other end, telling me that you had delayed your return for twenty-four hours. Boy, was I ever upset! As I recall, I told you that I was expecting you home instead of a telephone call and that I was not only disappointed but mad and I wanted you "back home!" Then in a childish burst of temper and insecurity, generously blended with selfishness, I hung up.

You did arrive the next day, and in my childish, petty way I set about to punish you for doing such a dastardly thing. Come to think about it, I'm not certain that I ever properly apologized for acting like such a complete boor. For fear that I didn't, I'm really sorry, Sugar Babe. Will you forgive me?

Your ever-lovin' husband,

HILARY

Thought: *If you really love someone, it's not that hard to make the first move to make up. It is a sign of maturity and, after all, the marriage you make happier is your own!*

WHAT TO DO WHEN CONFLICT ENTERS

Honey, *My* Honey,

There is *no* person as lucky or as blessed as I am to have such a husband as you. You are so loving, kind, considerate, and compassionate, and I love you so much — in every way possible.

I have felt so badly about what I did yesterday (the incident about the groceries), and there you were — only thinking about *my* needs. I should have remembered your speaking engagement and all your other commitments. Please forgive me and I *will* be less selfish — 'cause you're the most important person in the world to me and I *never* want to hurt you or cause a conflict.

I just love you so much and I'm so happy with my own Honey!

SUGAR BABY

P.S.   *The "incident" was just that — an incident. But incidents grow and fester if not dealt with. How grateful I am that the Redhead stopped this one dead in its tracks!*

DATING

Dear Suzan, Chad, Julie, Jim, and all other parents of dating daughters,

I know it's a long time before your daughters start their dating lives, but I wanted to offer a thought or two well in advance of the event.

I particularly want to caution you about permitting your daughters to date older boys, especially when your girls are in the ninth and tenth grades. If a senior develops an interest in one of them at that age, you're playing with real fire—according to my psychiatrist friend, the late John Kozek—if the relationship is permitted to develop.

The reason is two-fold. First, a younger girl is generally flattered that a senior would find her attractive. As a result, she might go overboard to keep him interested. Realistically, he is more socially poised and experienced. Second, in all too many cases the senior boy is interested in a freshman or sophomore girl because of a lack of success in dating girls his own age. To salvage his ego, he seeks the company of a younger girl. He might also visualize her as "easy pickin's" and a chance to assert his maleness.

Chances are good that he suffers from a poor self-image and is seeking confirmation of his sexuality by acquiring a date with any pretty girl, regardless of age. This is not true in all cases, but it is true too often. At age fifteen, which your daughters will be at that time, they will have plenty of years and boys in front of them. Play it safe and encourage (make that *require*) them to date boys of their own age.

Love,

DAD

P.S. *Evidence is solid that any "date," beyond a*
chaperoned party or a double-date for church
or school activities under controlled condi-
tions, until the girls (and guys) are at least
sixteen years old is not in their best interests.

WILL ALL THE "GOOD BOYS" REALLY BE GONE?

Dear Suzan, and all courting teenagers,

In a lifetime many things happen that parents, unfortunately, do not record, so they are lost forever. Some are best
forgotten but it would be nice to be able to recall all the
beautiful and pleasant memories. I will never forget one
incident that took place when you were a teenager. You
might remember it, Doll. As a matter of fact, I'm sure you do.
One afternoon after school you wanted to go with some of
your classmates to a particular place. I emphatically said
"no." Understandably, you wanted to know why. I explained
it was the wrong place with the wrong group. You retorted,
"Well, everybody else is going!" (So far I'll bet our conversation sounds familiar to millions of parents.)

To this I responded, "Now, Doll, you know perfectly good
and well that would not be a reason for you to go." Now with
your lips quivering slightly you said, "Why?" I replied that it
was the wrong place at the wrong time with the wrong people.
Somewhat upset, you insisted, "But, Dad, if I don't go out
with the boys and girls, all of the 'good' boys will be gone!"
(As an aside, Doll, I know you now know that all of the "good"
boys were not "gone." At that very moment Chad was waiting

in the wings to meet and marry you.) At any rate, I assured you that all of the "good" boys would not be gone. Again you responded in anger and frustration, wanting—even demanding—a clearer explanation of why you couldn't go.

I answered this by saying I was certain your friends wanted to be with you. I said, however, that historically our friends often have a tendency to change some of their values and even some of their friends'. I acknowledged that you loved your friends and they probably loved you, but their love could change at a whim or because of an incident. I stressed the love your mother and I felt for you would never change. I told you we loved you far too much to permit you to jeopardize either your health or your reputation by going to the place you named. You quietly stood there for a few seconds with your lips quivering and the trace of a few tears in your eyes. Then you almost jumped forward, hugged my neck, gave me a big kiss and said, "Thank you Daddy, I really didn't want to go anyhow!"

Now Doll, I have no earthly idea what you told your friends. You might well have told them your Daddy was old-fashioned and just didn't understand. But that's beside the point. As a parent I did what I honestly felt was best for you, and you apparently felt the same way. That's just one of the reasons I love you so much.

Your ever-lovin' Dad

Message: *Our kids constantly test us to see if we love them enough to say "no" when it would be much easier to say "yes." After all, real love is doing what is best for the child, not necessarily what the child wants.*

SOAP OPERAS ARE
A MORAL CESSPOOL

Dear Family (and all courting teenagers),

As I was dressing this morning I was watching "The Today Show," and during one of the commercial breaks I saw an advertisement for a soap opera. Soap operas are one of my pet peeves because I do not believe anyone can consistently watch them and maintain a healthy, optimistic, moral outlook on life. The reason is simple. Soap operas present a completely unrealistic, negative, and immoral outlook on life. They present their stories in such a persuasive, addictive format that viewers literally get hooked on them. They become so involved that they think of the people on the soaps as real people, not actors playing roles.

Two examples: A friend of mine, formerly with CBS, told me that when one of the major stars in one of the soaps got married on the show, the star received a great many wedding gifts—some of them very expensive (fine china, cookware, and crystal) from viewers. In another episode, one of the stars was killed off and over a hundred people marched in protest on the studios, demanding that the star be resurrected and brought back onto the program. I submit for your consideration a weekly condensation of one of the soaps:

> Luke learned that Natalie and her ex-husband, Marty Monroe, split up because of her anti-American politics. Natalie was accidentally shot when Connie caught her searching Rob's pad for the disc microfilm. At the hospital Connie wrongly identified Natalie as "The Mole." Greg injects air into Natalie's veins, knowing it will kill her instantly. Leslie wins money at the casino and seems to have caught the "Gambling Bug." Blackie is attracted to Cooper but Lou turns on the charm to win him back. Scotty schemed to enter the mayoral race, learning that Jackie printed Ruby and Bobbi's "rap sheets." Scotty blackmailed Jackie to write a "puff piece" news story about him.

Changa asked Brian to accept a Social Services job in Africa. Bobbi suspected she's pregnant. Brock says the last thing he wants is more kids.

In one week this particular soap dealt with *divorce, anti-American politics, accidental shooting, breaking and entering, mistaken identification, murder, gambling, addiction, homosexuality, scheming, subterfuge, blackmail,* and *unwanted pregnancy.* Question: How many of these would you identify as positive?

If you think I overstate the case, tune in on any one of them and here's what you'll find *every* time: The hero and the heroine, the junior hero and the junior heroine, the junior-junior hero and the junior-junior heroine, and the junior-junior-junior hero and the junior-junior-junior heroine are all either *in trouble, headed for trouble,* or they just got *out of trouble.* Now, kids, life might be tough, but it's not *that* tough!

Professor Bradley Greenberg says, "Soap operas may be a major force in the transmission of values and life styles and sexual information to youthful viewers. In general, kids will find that the world consists chiefly of doctors and lawyers, illegitimate children, people having abortions or nervous breakdowns, and most of all, people having illicit sex ranging from fornication and adultery to incest and homosexuality. The values and life styles portrayed on the soaps are not the ones associated with integrity, fidelity, wholesomeness, and sex within the confines of marriage."

The "soaps" are particularly damaging to impressionable teenagers because they present in a convincing manner the concept that sexual relationships between unmarried people are fine, even desirable, if the relationship is "meaningful." *Nothing* could be further from the truth!

In my opinion, it is a virtual impossibility to watch the soaps on a daily basis and remain optimistic *and* morally sound. The soaps are just one of the reasons you should spend minimal time in front of the television, and rarely or never should parents leave young children unattended in front of a television set.

Possibly one of the most alarming developments, one that is fraught with peril, has been the advent of the video music channels. On a recent flight, psychologist Denis Waitley expressed to me his deep concern over this intrusion into our homes. I share his concern.

The video music channels (offered by independent producers and the major networks) introduce background pictures to the music to which our young people are listening. Many of us have been concerned, based on solid evidence, that rock and roll, heavy metal and punk rock, acid rock, and much of the country and western tunes really amount to little more than pornography set to music. This music often contains messages openly advocating rebellion, fornication, adultery, homosexuality, and even incest and intercourse with the dead. As horrible as these were on radio and cassette recordings, the possible damage of video music is infinitely greater.

According to Dr. Waitley, when youngsters are viewing or dancing to these tunes in front of their television sets, they also are seeing the video inserts depicting the songs. In addition to the conscious bombardment of bizarre antics performed by our teenagers' heroes and heroines, there is the subconscious programming of subliminal implants, showing every wild, way-out act involving violence, deviant lifestyles, ghoulish graveyard scenes, incredible acts of sexual misconduct, and sado-masochism. If repeated viewing of a sixty-second commercial can sell you a product, isn't it reasonable to suspect that repeated viewing of a "video musical drama" can sell your kids a value system?

According to Dr. Waitley, when a youngster repeatedly views "music TV" in which some of the individual productions cost over a million dollars to make and run as long as fourteen minutes *each*, his or her behavior can be adversely affected permanently. Additionally, these subliminal implants literally take away or curtail the youngster's ability to fully utilize his or her own imagination for creative purposes. It's one thing to hear the words; it's something altogether different to hear the words and see the appalling scenes that accompany them. I am absolutely convinced that television sets with a video music channel on them, as well as many of the cable channels that show the same materials, are a moral threat of incredible proportions to the family. It also represents a threat of considerable magnitude to the mental growth and development of the viewers.

One of the great things about America is that we have the freedom to choose. I personally have no idea what your response to this particular message might be, but this I do know: If I were a young man today, just starting my family, I would make every effort to provide for them; but one of the things I definitely would not provide would be a television set. On balance, I believe that in the process of raising our children today the parents have a much better chance of raising happy, successful, well-adjusted children without a television set than they do with one. In case you are wondering how you are going to "keep up with things," let me point out that a recent study revealed that one issue of the typical daily newspaper contains more news than is shown on television in an average week.

Love,

DAD

PRE-MARITAL SEX

Dear Tom (and all other courting teenagers),

Well, that was quite a weekend we had, wasn't it, Son? It was great to get off, just the two of us. We had a chance to play a lot of golf and I really enjoyed that. Most of all, though, I enjoyed being with you and having those long talks. The purpose of this letter is to rehash and evaluate what was said and the reason for the trip. I want to put this in writing to keep things in perspective, because some very significant areas were discussed, which could have an impact on your life.

To begin with, the idea came from reading Christian psychologist Dr. James Dobson's books. He suggests that fathers should take off on long weekends with their sons and really talk to them about life, but mostly about their relationships with members of the opposite sex. Fortunately, Son, you and I have talked all of your life and have spent a lot of time together, so the subject matter was easy to cover and I felt comfortable in the conversation. Apparently you did, too. I felt that as you approached your seventeenth birthday it would be an ideal time because you had started dating a mighty pretty little girl. Your relationship with her was getting beyond the casual stage, so I wanted to touch some bases and cover some ground that had, in one form or another, been covered earlier.

As you know, I do not believe in the "double standard" and am appalled at the thought that some parents are of the opinion that it's permissible for their sons to get involved in premarital sex but not right for their daughters. Of course, the Bible says that marriage is the only condition where sex is permitted.

As you might recall, I pointed out that it was definitely best for you and for the girl to be very careful in your relationship. I specifically shared with you the belief that premarital sex was not in the best interests of either of you. There are many reasons for this besides the fact that God says "no." There are practical reasons, Son, like the possibility of pregnancy, venereal disease, getting caught and embarrassed, and the destruction of your moral values. But it goes considerably beyond that. The physical drive and attraction between teenagers is enormously strong. Some say it is *the* strongest at ages sixteen, seventeen, and eighteen.

I pointed out, Son, that if you refrain from sex at this time in your life, when your physiological desires are at their height, you will have demonstrated discipline, restraint, trust, and respect, all of which are critical to a successful marriage. Here's why: In marriage you and your wife will normally see each other almost every day, but there are still those periods when you will be apart. You may be on a business trip, or one of you may be physically ill, or your wife might be carrying your child. If you have refrained from an immoral act during your youth, you will have undergone the best training and discipline for restraining yourself from immoral acts during your marriage.

I say "immoral" because premarital sex is immoral, regardless of what the current thinking might be. Being in love constitutes no grounds and is certainly no condition for premarital sex. The *only* condition for a sexual relationship is marriage. A sexual relationship other than with your husband or wife is either perversion, adultery, or fornication—all sins—*period.*

As you know, Son, one of the most important factors in a successful marriage is mutual trust. I know you've heard me say this many times, but it's very comforting to know that when I leave home I never have to worry about your mother being anything less than 100 percent loyal to me. Of course, she has the same assurance that I'm going to be 100 percent loyal to her. That's awfully nice, Son, because it gives each of us a tremendous feeling of security, knowing there is that one who loves and trusts us above all others.

As strange as it might sound initially, one of the best reasons for refraining from premarital sex is that it eliminates any chance you have of really getting to know the girl you are courting. Once you start a sexual relationship, that is *all* you and the girl will think about or plan for. You will plot, scheme, maneuver, manipulate, and otherwise move heaven and earth to find the time and place for a sexual rendezvous.

It effectively ends 90 percent of the serious discussions between you. You won't cover the thousand-and-one little things and the dozens of *big* things that will make or break a marriage. I mean things like these: "Do we have children, and if so, how many? Which set of parents do we spend Thanksgiving, Christmas, Mother's Day, and Father's Day with, or do we stay home? Will the wife work and if so, for how long? If "yes," will she continue to work after a family has been started? What is the relative spending-saving philosophy? What about church—will you attend his, hers, or neither?" There are many other such questions, Son, but I hope you are getting the idea that these questions should have mutually acceptable answers *before* the wedding bells ring.

Another practical reason for no premarital sex and for not living together before marriage is that the divorce rate for those who do so is higher than for those who play it straight before marriage. Oh, I know that some of the shallow, tongue-in-cheek philosophers of the modern set would argue that they wouldn't "buy a car without trying it out," so they don't want a mate they haven't "tried out." What they don't realize is that cars have no moral values or consciences. Besides, it is a fact that when you drive that car out of the showroom its value drops substantially. It's also true, Son, that if you "try out" a girl before marriage, her value—to herself *and* to you—will go down. It's equally true that your value to yourself *and* to her will also go down. How tragic.

There's yet another reason, Son. If you get involved in premarital sex and later discover that you really are not meant for each other, it will be more difficult to part company. On the other hand, if there are no guilt-strings attached because of a sexual relationship, it will be much easier for both of you to walk away with a clear conscience and with your heads held high.

In addition, there is the fact that if you truly love the girl, get involved with her sexually, and later marry her, you will have set yourself up for future problems. My friends who counsel married people tell me that the two things they deal with the most are, first, wives who desperately wish their husbands would assume their position as the spiritual leader in the home and, second, men and women who indulged in premarital sex and are consumed with guilt because of it. This leads to a higher percentage of frigidity or impotence among those who indulged in premarital sex than among those who refrained and saved God's special gift for the marriage bed.

There is yet another real danger, and that's the fact that you might develop a satisfactory, even exciting, sexual relationship with a girl, but for many reasons you do not marry her. Later, you might find and marry the girl God has chosen for you. Now suppose this special girl has every single quality important in a wife but the two of you are not as sexually compatible as you were with the girl you did not marry. This could create a problem, Son, which you would never have had if you had simply waited, in obedience to God's command to indulge in no sexual activity until after you are married.

Many young people today are getting married to someone they neither love nor respect. When I was growing up back in the late 1930s and 1940s, we called them "shotgun weddings" because the father of the bride did put enormous pressure on

the boy who got his daughter in "trouble." Today some people
laugh about this and see nothing really wrong with premarital sex, which often leads to unwanted children who, in turn, often become abused children.

As it developed, Son, you are no longer dating that girl because, for whatever reason, the two of you did not hit it off over the long haul. It's really nice to know that neither of you were put in a position where there was any guilt involved. This makes it possible for you to be friends and to be able to visit and converse without those emotional guilt-strings tearing you apart. That relationship undoubtedly was a good one because it helped both of you to learn how to deal with members of the opposite sex while giving you a chance to grow and mature.

As you and I discussed, Son, there are some steps you can take to keep from falling into the trap of sexual involvement during these difficult times when you are seriously dating the one you sincerely feel you want to marry. I believe Josh McDowell expressed it best when he said that when you emotionally arouse an appetite you cannot Scripturally satisfy, you are guilty of fraud. To court under that restraint will require wisdom, faith, enormous restraint, and *careful planning.*

Plan to double-date as much as possible and spend time together in group activities. Plan to avoid watching movies or television programs that have passion as their theme and the "pleasure" of immorality as their message.

Start every date with prayer and end it with prayer. As you will recall, when your sister Julie had prayer with her date before and after their time together, his conduct on the date was substantially different.

Stay in God's Word. Dr. Paige Patterson, president of The Criswell Center for Biblical Studies, says the only way to protect yourself from sexual sin, whether you are a preacher or a layman, is to stay in God's Word. On a daily basis build a wall of strength based on God's Word around yourself. This is the way to protect yourself from Satan's fiery darts.

Avoid the temptation to park in some dark spot. Not only is it dangerous, but things have a tendency to get out of hand under those circumstances. Never go into either her house or yours unless other family members are present. No young man who *truly* loves his girlfriend and is using his head would put her in a position that makes her vulnerable — either to the criticism that *could* result from such indiscreet behavior or the temptation that *will* result from this behavior. Read *Love Must Be Tough,* by Dr. James Dobson, and you will understand why it's important to be tough on yourself before marriage. Yes, love and marriage to the right person is one of God's greatest blessings.

As you probably remember, Son, you thrilled me no end on that trip when you told me about your idea of heaven on earth. You said that it occurred when you saw your mother and me get aboard an airplane every November 26 for the three days we always set aside just for each other to celebrate our wedding anniversary. To tell you the truth, Son, that's my idea of heaven on earth, too! You know I am very much in love with your mother.

It always saddens me to hear people say they don't really enjoy spending that much time with their mates. To be completely honest, when your mother is out of my sight and then comes back, old Dad's heart still skips a beat. I find your mother to be the most fascinating and excitingly beautiful woman I've ever known.

Yes, that was quite a weekend you and I had, Son. We covered a lot of territory, and I was especially pleased when you suggested that we make it a tradition.

Love,

DAD

Thought: *Many parents talk to their children about the trivial things in life. Why not talk to them about the really important things?*

Fact: *The best sex education course you can possibly give your son or daughter is to let them observe their mother and father showing mutual love and respect for one another over a lifetime. Then Mom, in the natural course of events, shares the details of sex with her daughters, and Dad does the same thing with his sons.*

COURTSHIP: BEFORE
AND AFTER MARRIAGE

Dear Ziglar Children (and anyone else who plans to get married),

If you're married, I hope you are working at staying married. If you're unmarried, I hope you will pick the right mate when that time comes. There are many reasons for this, but the one I really want to talk about has to do with my grandchildren.

I know this might sound a little selfish, but my grandchildren are so much fun and bring such incredible joy into my life that it would break my heart to even think about grandchildren I might not get to enjoy. I go to many conventions and meetings where families are involved. On many occasions I meet "his kids," "her kids," and "their kids." Frequently I visit with parents and grandparents who get to see these children on weekends or special occasions. I often hear heartbreaking stories about families splitting and moving to other parts of the country and one parent and one set of grandparents being permanently separated from the children.

When this happens I can't help but think about the joy and thrill the absentee parent and grandparents will miss by not getting to share on a daily basis the pure exhilaration that goes with raising a child or a grandchild. They won't get to watch them grow and develop, to observe those first steps, to hear those first words, to watch them as they try to eat, to give them a bath, and to observe all the other "firsts" in their lives. That's one of the reasons your mother and I have put so much stress on dating the right person because if you "court" right, your chances of marrying right are dramatically increased.

By "courting" right I mean you should date someone with similar interests, religious beliefs, moral convictions, and backgrounds. The person you court should be someone you would be proud to present as the parent of your child. You should also be compatible *and* comfortable with the family of the person you are courting. As I mentioned earlier, you *do* marry the whole family. It is also extremely important that you spend a lot of time talking to each other. I can guarantee you that if you don't have a lot to talk about before the marriage, when each one of you is trying to sell the other one on the marriage idea, then you won't have anything to talk about after marriage.

On bended knees I *beg* you not to marry anyone with the idea that you are going to reform or change that person after the wedding. Remember, if your prospective mate won't change while trying to persuade you to get married, the message you deliver when you do marry is crystal clear. You love him and "bought" him as he is, and it's not necessary or even important to change after the marriage. If your beloved has a "slight" drinking problem ("Nothing serious, I can handle it," you are told) before marriage, you should expect a serious problem after marriage. If the prospective mate has a "slight" temper that gets a little out of hand during courtship, your chances of being physically abused after marriage are good.

Courtship and marriage is serious business. It involves you, your family, and the family God might bless you with, which is another reason we put so much emphasis on courtship before *and* after marriage. It is possible to marry the wrong person, treat him or her right, and have a workable marriage. It is also possible to marry the right person, treat him or her wrong, and create an unworkable marriage. With guidelines stated earlier, however, you might prevent an unhappy marriage.

Love,

DAD

> P.S. *The next letter offers a suggestion which, if you are married and the marriage is just "so-so," I hope you will take. If your marriage is good and you want to make it better, or if it's super and you want to make it double-super, I also urge you to follow through on the suggestion.*

COMMUNICATIONS: THE KEY TO FAMILY LOVE

Dear Sugar Baby, and everybody else interested in a better marriage,

When people started suggesting that you and I should go to Christian Marriage Encounter, I thought it was a waste of time to take such an unnecessary step. I reasoned that no one could possibly make our marriage any better. So many people made the suggestion, however, that finally the message got through. And, as you know, we had that beautiful weekend experience—and what an experience it was!

How marvelous it was to have all those hours together, sharing and drawing closer and closer. Our experience was so good we decided to send any of our company people who wanted to go to Christian Marriage Encounter at our expense.

One of the big things we learned was communication. Actually, that's what this book is about—how to communicate. That's not to say, Sweetheart, that I think you and I have all the answers, but I do truly feel that most of the time we communicate our love to each other in a loving, meaningful way. Sure do love you.

ZIG

Thought: *A wise man once said that "They do not love who do not show their love." I'm not certain that's completely true, but I do believe that if a person truly loves someone he or she will take whatever steps are necessary to learn how to communicate that love by showing a deep and sincere interest in the things his or her mate is interested in.*

Write: *Christian Marriage Encounter*
Post Office Box 1342
Colorado Springs, Colorado 80901

HELP NEEDED

Dear Sugar Baby, and all other back-seat drivers,

Despite the fact that many years ago I accepted the idea that you were always going to "help me drive," I still lapse into periods when I "forget" and try to do the driving myself.

Never will I forget the day we were driving on the access road at North Central Expressway. The yield sign was very much in evidence and I knew I was supposed to stop for the traffic coming off the expressway. As we neared the exit, a car leaving Central Expressway was going extremely slow, and I was confident the driver did not realize he had the right-of-way. Actually, the car was in the process of stopping (in retrospect, it might have been because he wasn't sure I was going to stop), so I kept going. The following dialogue was the result:

Sugar Baby: "Zig, we're supposed to yield." Zig: "I know" (as I kept going). Sugar Baby: "Zig, we are supposed to yield." Since the other car had completely stopped, in a very gruff, belligerent voice I declared, "Sweetheart, I know it. But can't you see that the other car has stopped?"

At that moment there was very little love in the inflection of my voice or in my words. So the question is, what did you do? The answer is, you handled it in the typical Sugar Baby way. You looked at me, smiled, and with that beautiful twinkle in your eye said, "Now, Honey, you know long ago we both decided that I was always going to help you drive and it's not going to do you any good to get mad at me at this stage of the game."

That's not quite fair, Sweetheart. How in the world could I possibly resist an approach like that? That's just one more of the 11,986 reasons I love you.

Your ever-lovin' husband,

ZIG

Thought: *The Bible certainly hit this one on the head: "A soft answer turneth away wrath."*

Fact: *It takes two to fight or argue.*

Procedure: *The next time your mate gets out of sorts with you and flies off the handle, why not take the Sugar Baby approach and love him or her enough to forgive and start pouring some healing oil on the troubled waters.*

SEX EDUCATION

Dear Julie, Suzie, and all other parents,

As you have learned, your mother and I try to avoid telling you how to raise your children. However, I want to put something in the record regarding their sex education in the hope you will think it is valid and that other parents will perhaps profit from the comments.

Let me encourage you girls never to permit your children to take a sex education course in the public schools. If you will read page 69 of the September 7, 1981, issue of *Time* magazine, you will clearly understand why. That might be the most frightening single page I've ever read in a magazine. It discusses sex education, but more importantly it discusses sex educators. The article deals at some length with Dr. Mary Calderone, who was formerly in charge of SIECUS (Sex Information and Education Council for the United States), and sex educators from Sweden and Denmark.

Some of these good people from Sweden and Denmark, where liberalism abounds, are of the opinion that young children should not only be permitted to indulge in sex, but should actually be encouraged to do so. They also feel that incest should be taken off the statute books as a crime because, after all, as they express it, a six-year-old can say "no." That's sick.

Now the reason I'm concerned about this is the fact that SIECUS is a principal supplier of the sex information taught in the schools. To be completely candid, I do not want a homosexual or an immoral heterosexual teaching my grandchildren. To call a spade a spade, the teacher, whether good, bad, or indifferent, teaches what he or she *is*. As God tells us in Luke 6:40, "A student is not above his teacher: but everyone who is fully trained will be like his teacher" (NIV). How *frightening*, if the teacher is the wrong kind of role model; how *exciting*, if the teacher is the right kind of role model!

Among other things, the materials supplied by SIECUS identify homosexuality as an acceptable alternate lifestyle and discuss abortion as another means of birth control. They often teach that premarital sex is fine as long as it fits your value system or is a "meaningful relationship." They make no effort to sell the idea that the moral life is the better life.

I encourage you to read *The Heart Does Not Speak English*, by Dr. William McGrath, a psychiatrist from Phoenix, Arizona. Dr. McGrath points out that between the ages of approximately five to adolescence a period of latent development exists in our children. He says that during that period of time little boys should learn how to get along with little boys, play little boy games, and learn what it is to be a little boy. Little girls should play little girl games, learn how to get along with little girls, and learn what it is to be a little girl. He points out that any artificial sexual stimulation of a youngster during this critical period of time, whether it is via the media, personal experience, or sex education classes, frequently does irreparable damage to the child.

According to Dr. McGrath, premature stimulation makes children skip a period of growth that is vitally important. Each period of life prepares a person for the next period, and if you skip a period you never make it up. This is one of the reasons we have so many young men and women, twenty-five and thirty years old, who are moving back home with their parents, or who are at least partially supported by their parents. They never matured; they skipped a vital period of growth. That's the reason I'm concerned, girls, and address the subject now.

As you know, your Dad is—according to modern standards—kind of old-fashioned, inasmuch as I believe in the old standards of marriage, morality, and fidelity. There are numerous reasons for this, which we've discussed. One of them has to do with the productivity of our children. Survey after survey of the kids on various Who's Who lists conclusively prove that the top students, be they male or female, overwhelmingly have faith in God, believe in sexual abstinence until after marriage, do not smoke pot, nor drink alcohol.

When you analyze this, it makes sense that the top students would have those values. Dealing only with sex at the moment, the young boy or girl who does not indulge in sex is in no danger of catching a venereal disease (which is rampant in today's society), there's no possibility of pregnancy with an illegitimate birth, a premature, unwanted, undesirable marriage, or an abortion as the result. The youngster who practices sexual morality can concentrate on growing up and preparing for life so he or she will be ready for a job and a family later in life.

Many sex education advocates contend that with all the illegitimate births, we need to "educate" youngsters on birth control. Actually, in Sweden, Denmark, and the United States, public school sex education always brings an increase in premarital sex, venereal disease, abortion, and illegitimate births.

I know this is a heavy load for one letter, so I'll shut 'er down. Just want you to know I am concerned about this, that I love you deeply, and that I love those beautiful grandchildren and obviously want the best for all of you.

Love,

DAD

Thought: *We don't need sex education or birth control for our young. We need moral education on self-control.*

PROPER COURTSHIP LEADS TO PROPER MARRIAGE

Dear Tom,

From time to time you've asked about courting and how you can reduce the margin for error in selecting a wife. I have some definite ideas I'd like to share with you. We've talked about most of them, but I wanted to put this in the official record book.

First of all, Son, I would suggest that, as a practical matter, you do not date a girl you would be unwilling to marry. Let me tell you why. We are emotional by nature, and many times we're unable to separate fact from fiction and head from heart. It could be that you might date a girl who would be completely unsuitable as your wife, but who might appear to be "fun" for a few dates. There is always the danger that you might fall in love with her and she with you. If you follow the Scriptures that admonish you not to be unequally yoked, then this could present some real problems. If you didn't marry her, both of you would end up with broken hearts. Needless to say, this would not be fair to either one of you. If you decided to go ahead with a marriage, which obviously was not proper, that would be even more tragic. Not only would your own two hearts be broken, but both families' and any children who resulted from the marriage would be the victims of the mistake.

John Benton's book, *Do You Know Where Your Children Are?*, really has some thought-provokers along these lines. John pointed out something I had not considered as he discussed marrying someone from a different culture. He pointed out that the Bible does not say anything against it, and reminded us that Moses married a woman of a different race.

Scripturally I find no evidence that God says "no." However, as John Benton pointed out, you need to consider what the responses of other people would be to the marriage. He uses an exaggerated example and says that if you married a man or a woman who weighed five hundred pounds, it would obviously be an individual who was dramatically "different." If you married someone who was seven feet tall or four feet tall, people would notice and point you out. Benton says you've got to ask yourself if you could handle this attention. It's worth thinking about because if you marry someone who is "different," you are going to be subjected to a lot of attention.

One of the things that you'll certainly want to take into account, Son, is the fact that, contrary to what some people say, you really do marry the whole family. I think one of the reasons your mother and I have gotten along so well and love each other as much as we do is because our backgrounds are so similar. She comes from a strong Christian family and so do I. She was raised during the Depression and so was I. She was brought up in the church and so was I. She lost her dad at a very early age and so did I. She's from a reasonably large family and I'm from a big family. This gave us a lot of things in common.

I fell more deeply in love with her and got more excited about becoming a permanent part of her life as I came to know her mother and the rest of her family. I'm certain she came to love me more as she came to know my mother and the rest of my family. In short, Son, her family and mine "fit." This certainly has come in handy over the years because our families were always more than welcome in one another's homes. It has been a good relationship and has added stability to our marriage. You'll want to consider these things when you start looking for a bride or date a girl more than four or five times.

There are other factors, too, Son. When you visit in your girlfriend's home over a period of time, you will discover that the guards come down and everyone acts in a normal manner, so you will see how the family really lives. You will find out if she helps her mother around the house; if she does little things like mending her own dresses and keeping her own room clean; whether she wants to serve or be served; and how she gets along with the other members of her family.

Most of all, you'll be able to see how she treats her dad, because ultimately, Son, that's about the way she's going to treat you. If she's thoughtful, considerate, and shows respect to him, you can pretty well be assured that she's going to be thoughtful, considerate, and respectful of you. If she's critical and disrespectful to him, you can be pretty well assured that you will ultimately be treated the same way.

The advantage of having her come to visit you and your family is she'll get to know all of us, including our strong and weak points. She'll find out how you treat your mother and how you deal with your dad. She'll find out how you get along with other members of the family and whether or not you carry your load. Lots of little things that just don't come out in a day or a week or a month will emerge over a period of time.

You can also discover what kind of restrictions her parents place on her. If they let her stay out as long as she wishes, then that really is a strike against the family because young people today need some restraints. You'll have certain restraints, too, Son, as long as you live under our roof. There'll be certain things you can and cannot do and certain times to come home. I think we're loving and fair, but as you know, we do not tolerate all-night hours or drugs or alcohol. We're grateful you never presented a problem with those things.

I realize this is a lengthy letter, but the subject matter is truly serious. I'm sure you and I will be talking about this from time to time over these next few years. One of the things I like best about you as a son is that we can talk about anything and everything.

Love,

DAD

Thought: *Marriage is serious, so preparation for it should be serious.*

MARRIAGE IS MY GOAL

Dear Tom (and every other young man contemplating marriage),

It's amazing, but when I started these letters you were just four years old, and now you're eighteen and talking about marriage. That's completely understandable, Son, though I must confess that when I first heard the word "marriage" from you my first feeling was that you were far too young. Then I remembered that when I was eighteen I was madly in love with your mother and we were talking about marriage. However, there were some things we had to do before we could get married, just as there are some goals you need to reach before you can take that giant step.

In my case, I was in the Navy, and marriage would have forced me to resign from the Naval Air Force training program. Combine that with the fact that your mother was only sixteen and it's easy to understand why we waited. Her mother would have been a powerful deterrent and I wanted her on my side! Additionally, your mom wasn't ready and although I didn't realize it, I wasn't either.

At this stage of the game, Son, there are some substantial obstacles standing between you and the *Wedding March.* You are aware of most of them, but let me touch on a few things you are familiar with and a few which perhaps you have not considered. In addition, perhaps I can share with you some ideas as to how you can set a realistic date to reach this goal, as well as the necessary steps to get there.

To begin with, there is college, to which you are committed to finish. I know you agree that in the modern world a good education is important. It puts you in a better position to financially provide for your family. If the marriage should be blessed with children, you will be better prepared to educate those children. In short, one major goal should be the completion of college.

I know that four years seems like a long time, but believe me, Son, when you're busy and working toward an objective, the time will pass. In the meantime, it gives both of you enough time to make certain that each of you is marrying the right person.

Generally speaking, when someone tells me he's set a goal to get married by a specific date, I'm inclined to encourage him not to set that kind of goal unless he is already courting that right person. At this point you seem to be quite confident you have found that girl, so now you need to get out your Goal Planner and work through all the steps.

Since marriage is your goal, you need to set a date, but that date is dependent upon the reaching of two other intermediate or companion goals. One of these goals is the completion of your college education, as I have mentioned. This can be done in as little as two and one-half years, or you can go four or five years. A companion goal should be a financial one, because no mature individual who truly loves his bride-to-be would take her on the sea of matrimony unless he can offer her at least a small financial life raft. That doesn't mean you need a hefty bank account, but it does mean that you should be financially responsible and have a dependable income.

Income is important, Son, and I encourage you to make your financial plans so that should children come earlier than planned your income alone would be adequate to cover your needs. Chances are excellent that you will plan to delay the family, but as you know, sometimes unplanned events do take place. If you make your plans based on the wife's income, you could be in for some rude surprises.

Now, let's see where we are. We've identified the goal, and we've listed at least two of the obstacles that stand between you and that goal. Now you need to develop a plan of action to reach the financial goal. That's pretty involved, Son, because it includes budget, discipline, job acquisition, and other things as well. We'll have a chance to talk about that one a lot, but you need to start the thought process now.

The third obstacle could well be the family of the bride-to-be. You must convince them that you're the right young man for their daughter's hand. Your mother and I are obviously convinced that you can handle that assignment. You are persuasive and, more importantly, you are a bright, morally sound, dedicated Christian, which means you've got lots going for you and even more going with you.

Your biggest obstacle is the one that prevents most people from reaching their goals. I speak of personal discipline. When you are courting and in love, the natural tendency is to shower gifts and entertainment on the one you love. This is especially true of those who are loving and giving, which accurately describes you. You will be tempted to buy loving gifts, send flowers, and go to nice restaurants. In short, you will want to entertain your bride-to-be in a spectacular fashion. That's not all bad, Son, but the question you must ask is, "Will this particular move help us reach our goal more quickly and be in our long-range best interests?"

"Should I spend thirty dollars tonight, which I had to work several hours to acquire, for a movie and a nice dinner, or should we schedule our time so that we can catch an afternoon matinee and be content with a hamburger?" The difference between ten dollars and thirty dollars when you multiply it many times over a four-year stretch is substantial.

It will represent the difference in buying your furniture versus having to rent a furnished apartment. You will have to decide whether to spend three dollars on a phone call every night or write a nice, long letter, reserving phone calls for after 11 P.M. once each week. You'll have to decide whether to invest in name-brand clothes to satisfy an ego trip or to buy adequate clothes on sale. You will have to decide to spend seven dollars for a haircut or fifteen dollars for a hair style. It's more than just a cliche that in order to have the money you want, you must first manage the money you have. That's not just heavy, Son, it is true, because at today's prices you can squander twenty-five dollars a week without materially changing your enjoyment, your appearance, or your future. Twenty-five dollars a week *saved* will give you a nest egg of over five thousand dollars, not counting interest, in four years.

What this really boils down to is, are you interested in pleasure or happiness? Pleasure is something all of us enjoy and in which many of us are inclined to indulge from time to time. However, in the final analysis, you will need to decide whether or not you wish to *spend* your money on short-term pleasures or *invest* that money in long-term happiness.

These are decisions you haven't really dealt with on such a serious matter. However, you need to start now to exercise the necessary discipline to insure reaching those long-range goals. As you get serious about this, you will need to make a number of adjustments along the way. However, as your Uncle Judge Ziglar would say, "You don't change your decision to go—you just change your direction to get there."

If your long-range objective is to get married, that goal can remain firm, but the road to get there could change. Example: You might initially decide to reach the preliminary goal of graduating in three years but soon discover that the work and study load make it impossible for you to keep the level of grades you have always maintained. With this new awareness, you may decide to drop some semester hours and delay the graduation date. You will have changed your plan of action but your goal will remain the same.

One thing you need to keep firmly in your mind is why you want to reach any objective. At the moment, as it relates to the marriage objective, you might respond, "I want to get married because I'm in love and believe I have found the girl who is right for me." There would be no argument from Dad, but you need to elaborate in order for it to become even more real and reachable.

I'm aware of the fact that for most eighteen-year-olds who are in love some of this sounds a bit calculating, but hear me out before you turn me off with the thought that "I'm in love and I want to get married. It's just that simple." That's the line of reasoning many people follow.

Unfortunately, many of the people who take that approach end up in the divorce courts. They often discover they either don't really have too much in common with the one they have chosen, or they haven't carefully planned to make their marriage a life-time arrangement. The net result is that once the bloom of the honeymoon is over, or when the inevitable difficulties arise, they quickly bail out of a marriage they should never have consummated. That's one of the reasons you need your own goals and your wife needs goals that are compatible with yours. One of the advantages of a long courtship is the fact that you will be able to really discover whether or not you love each other. You'll be able to intelligently decide whether your goals and temperaments are such that you will have an honest chance to be even happier with the marriage commitment twenty, thirty, or more years down the road.

You can rest assured that if you have to be going somewhere or doing something all the time, your love for that person is not really deep. Just enjoying being together could be the surest sign of love. Incidentally, that's one of the advantages of not having a lot of money during the courtship period. With money the tendency is to spend your time at shows, concerts, athletic events, restaurants, and parties. If you don't have any bucks in your pocket, you'll be more inclined to spend more time on the telephone talking with each other or taking long walks in the park or around the campus. By following this procedure you will learn whether or not you and your wife-to-be have enough in common to build a solid marriage.

Please don't misunderstand. We are people, not computers.

We are human beings, and the concept of matching each other step-by-step is not what I have in mind. It's simply that the more things you have in common, the greater your chances of being happy. When there are just the two of you in your little apartment, the cupboard is bare, the bank book is shot, and you are in danger of having the heat turned off, that's when your careful selection and planning will really pay off. Then you'll discover what a blessed couple you are to have each other. That's love, Son. That's real love. It might not be what they make movies about, but this is what makes life beautiful and meaningful.

As I look back on my relationship with your mother, I realize that some of our happiest moments together were those times when we had to scrape and struggle for everything we had. When we had our little spats it was all those things we had in common that made us know any disagreements we had were minor and would be quickly resolved. I can say with reasonable certainty that neither your mother nor I ever seriously thought about terminating our relationship. If either one of us did it was a fleeting thought that quickly left our minds. We had chosen carefully and had made our commitments. How grateful I am because our life together gets better and better. It's true. Love and marriage—to the right one—is one of God's richest blessings.

As I indicated earlier, all of this might sound a little heavy. It might even be more than you wanted to hear on the subject, but I'm going to encourage you, Son, to keep your copy of this book on hand so that on a regular basis you can read this section. This way you will be reminded of the goals you're setting and why you want to reach them.

Marriage really is a beautiful objective. As you know, Christ performed His first miracle at a wedding feast, thus stamping His seal of approval on marriage for all time. As you also know, your mother and I have thoroughly enjoyed our marriage. To be candid, it probably has not been as good as you and your sisters have viewed it because we simply have not paraded our differences in front of you or anybody else. However, I can honestly say that our marriage has been the most important thing in my life outside of my faith in our Lord. I look forward every day to spending time with your mother, and I'm excited about growing old with her and then spending eternity with her.

Yes, marriage can be beautiful, and I'm convinced it will be beautiful if it's based on three things. Number one, make Jesus Christ the center of your life and the head of your household. Number two, make certain you are not unequally yoked. Number three, you and your bride-to-be must court each other as carefully *after* you are married as you did before you got married.

God bless you, Son. He wants to and will if you stay in His will.

Love,

DAD

REAL LOVE GROWS AND GROWS

Dear Sugar Baby,

It shouldn't surprise you when I say that I want to go on living with you because of the total love I have for you. I could not conceive of life without you. The metamorphosis you have gone through in the past few years has truly been beautiful. Your perception and growth, combined with your commitment spiritually, has been astonishing in many ways. Your business maturity and judgment have grown tremendously. Your confidence and self-image have skyrocketed. You're even friendlier and reach out verbally and physically to touch me more often.

All of this really says that the past and all our experiences have been leading up to now. I believe our life will progressively grow more stimulating and rewarding. I see us right now as approaching high noon in our lives, with everything getting better and better. Then I see us totally enjoying a life of love and excitement for many, many more years. I see a beautiful sunset lasting a long time, but I see no dusk or darkness. I want to keep on living with you because I truly believe you are the perfect help-mate. You meet all my physical, spiritual, and emotional needs as a wife. I love to be with you whether it's in church, out to dinner, on a trip, taking a walk, or whatever.

I suppose my greatest thrill comes when you are with me on speaking engagements and they bring you on stage with me and everyone can see my Redhead—the Sugar Baby. I love to introduce you to those people who know what you mean to me. I always feel a little like the cat who swallowed the canary as, in essence, I can say to them with that introduction, "See, I told you she was special!" In case you're missing the point of all this, Sugar Baby, I love you and am terribly proud to be able to introduce you as my wife. That way people can know where I get my support and help. Hopefully there will be other husbands and wives who will see that if they will love and support their mates, both will win—and be happier in the process.

Your ever-lovin' husband,

ZIG

IS ANYTHING
REALLY FREE?

Dear Family (and everybody else),

Well, our weekend at the lake was one I will never forget. We had just moved into our beautiful new home and every member of my immediate family was there. It was really great playing golf with Tom, Chad, and Richard, and super-neat to be riding around the lake with you girls in the boat. It was exciting to show you around a place that had been a dream for your mother and me for a number of years. It was truly a time of rejoicing and an opportunity to express our gratitude to God for His goodness to us.

In retrospect, as I look back on the events leading up to the new home, including moving in, it really is exciting. This did not fully hit me until we'd been in the home about three weeks. At that point I realized that we had a rare opportunity.

Since this home is to be used primarily for a retreat and for me to do my writing, it hit me that we truly had a chance to start over.

By this I mean that all the furniture was new; the carpeting was new; the home was new; the appliances were new; as a matter of fact, everything in the home was new except my library, which I partially moved from Dallas for my research and writing.

How grateful I am that we had that "start over" opportunity. As I think back, however, I realize that the new start wasn't free. I was truly shocked at the price of some of the things. As you know, I was delighted with the work Bill Tenison did on our home. I feel that he delivered more than he had sold, but everything else seemed so enormously expensive. No, our beautiful new home wasn't free.

The only thing we have today that is truly free is our

salvation. It doesn't cost us anything. All we have to do is trust Jesus Christ as Lord and Savior, confess our sins, and He will invite us to spend eternity in Paradise with Him.

And yet our salvation was not free. God paid a terrible price for it. He sent His only begotten Son to earth as the supreme sacrifice for us. Christ paid an awful price. We'll never feel the pain of those nails going through our hands and feet; we'll never feel the agony of the cross as He paid for our sins. But the price was paid so that we might live with Him forever. How tragic, after the price our Lord paid, that many people will not accept that gift of salvation. How grateful I am that each one of you has come to know Christ on a personal basis and will spend eternity, along with your mother and me, with Him.

Love,

DAD

Dear Reader,

You undoubtedly noticed that most of this book has dealt with the positive aspects of life and the good parts of our family relationships. In my judgment, we place too much emphasis on the negative in our society, so I wanted to give you a more positive approach to family life and what it could be. To repeat what I said in the beginning, we as a family have had, and from time to time still have, some difficulties. However, I can't imagine a family who loves one another and shows that love any more than our family does. Without exception, when we greet each other it is with warmth and affection. The Redhead hugs and kisses everybody, the girls hug and kiss everybody, and all of us guys hug and kiss the girls and warmly shake hands and often hug each other.

Apparently our family has done *some* things right, and this book is written to help you establish some guidelines and perhaps some direction in making your family life more loving, beautiful, and meaningful.

I close with this poem which clearly and beautifully identifies my purpose in writing this book:

THE BRIDGE BUILDER

An old man going a lone highway
Came in the evening, cold and gray
To a chasm vast and deep and wide.
The old man crossed in the twilight dim,
The sullen stream had no fear for him,
But he stopped when safe on the other side
And built a bridge to span the tide.

"Old man," said a fellow pilgrim near,
"You're wasting your strength with building here;
Your journey will end with the ending day,
You never again will pass this way,
You've crossed the chasm deep and wide,
Why build you this bridge at evening tide?"

The builder lifted his old gray head,
"Good friend, in the path I have come," he said,
"There followeth after me today
A youth whose feet must pass this way.

This chasm which has been naught to me
To that fair-haired youth may a pitfall be.
He, too, must cross in the twilight dim,
Good friend, I am building this bridge for
him.

Will Allen Dromgoole

Yes, as a family we have crossed some bridges in our life together. It is my hope, prayer, and conviction that the suggestions and love in this book will provide for you a bridge that will enable you to build a more meaningful relationship with those you love.

ZIG ZIGLAR

EPILOGUE

On November 29, 1983, my wife and I flew to Lubbock, Texas, for a moving and significant event. James and Juanell Teague celebrated their twenty-fifth wedding anniversary by rededicating their lives to each other and to God. One of the highlights of my life was the invitation to participate in the ceremony. I am not a minister, but the Teagues and the Ziglars have been close friends for a long time, and they wanted me to "officially"—"unofficially"—officiate in this holy event.

During the months preceding the anniversary, I listened to a recording by my good friend, Dr. Richard Furman. In his recording, Dr. Furman described an insurance policy that gives a marriage four-hundred-to-one odds of being successful. I utilized the basic ideas in the insurance policy, rewrote it as a covenant, and used it as the central part of the ceremony.

The successful marriage is the bedrock of the family, and since the marriage of James and Juanell Teague is so successful and their rededication was so beautiful, I have taken the basic concepts of their covenant (which was personalized for their special occasion) and rewritten it to help meet the needs and ensure the marriages of others.

If you would like a copy of this covenant on parchment, suitable for framing, drop us a note at our corporate address: The Zig Ziglar Corporation, 13642 Omega at Alpha Roads, Dallas, Texas 75234, or call us at 1/800-527-0102 (in Texas 214/233-9191).

COVENANT

Because we, _____ and _____,
have chosen to become "one," we quite naturally want our
marriage to be successful, happy, and permanent.

To accomplish this objective, we individually and jointly
pledge to respect, encourage, and support each other as
individuals. We further agree to insure the success, happiness,
and permanence of our marriage by keeping the promises
stated in our marriage vows and in this sacred covenant.

Understanding that marriage is under attack and the family
is in trouble, we promise to demonstrate to the world that a
truly committed husband and wife, with God's help, can have
a beautiful marriage and grow in love for one another in the
process.

Accepting the fact that God is the Author of success in
marriage, and believing the best way to stay in His will is to
stay in His Word, we agree to seek His will and direction
every day by reading the Bible and humbling ourselves before Him in prayer.

Because God specifically promises, "For them that honor me
I will honor," we solemnly promise to honor God in every
phase of our individual lives as well as in our life together.

Knowing that the fellowship of believers gives encouragement to individuals and support to the family structure, we agree to make a maximum effort to attend worship services together each week.

Believing that marriage is ordained and blessed by God, we pledge our love and faithfulness to Him and to each other. Being aware of the frailties of man and recognizing the probability of falling short of this lofty objective, we further pledge to love, honor, and forgive one another even as God, for Christ's sake, has loved, honored, and forgiven us.

We thank God for bringing us together and ask Him in His Providence to keep His hand on our marriage and to heal any hurts we inflict upon one another. Because we now more completely commit this marriage to Jesus Christ, our faith assures us that under His watchcare, "the best is yet to be." We reverently enter this sacred covenant because we know these pledges and procedures will completely assure greater happiness and permanence of our "one love shared by two."

_____   _____